Phantasmagoria®: A Puzzle of Flesh

The Official Strategy Guide

Rick Barba

Prima Publishing
Rocklin, California
(916) 632-4400

Table of Contents

ACKNOWLEDGMENTS

It's just so horribly appropriate that I'm writing this Acknowledgments page on October 31, 1996—Halloween. My first thanks go to the people at Sierra who produced such a dream-haunting experience as *Phantasmagoria: A Puzzle of Flesh.*

In particular, thanks to Lorelei Shannon for writing and designing this creepily entertaining game, and for being so gracious with her time. Thanks also to Tammy Dargan for her liaison work on this project, and to Andy Hoyos for his last-minute help on some of the more perplexing elements of the beta software version of the game. Finally, thanks to Roberta Williams for inspiring and mentoring Sierra's talented crop of female game designers, such as Ms. Shannon and Jane Jensen. Computer gaming will get only better as more women become involved in the primary design process.

On the Prima side of things, my gratitude falls upon the usual suspects. Thanks to my project editor, Julie Asbury, for her expert guidance, support, camaraderie, and good humor; to Sam Mills for sharpening the prose and keeping the book elements tight and aligned, and to Connie Nixon for still another inspired design.

Introduction

Welcome to the official strategy guide for one of the most anticipated sequels in computer gaming history. The original *Phantasmagoria is* now one of the best-selling computer game titles of all time. It set new standards in interactive gaming with its stunning production values, its graphic (and I do mean *graphic*) innovations, and its chilling subject matter. Fans will be happy to know that *Phantasmagoria: A Puzzle of Flesh* pushes the gaming envelope still further in all of those areas.

Indeed, to say that *Phantasmagoria: A Puzzle of Flesh* breaks new ground in computer gaming might be an understatement. True fans of the horror genre will welcome the fact that this sequel pulls no punches in terms of intensity (at least in the "More Intense" version) or subject matter. Indeed, with its explicit themes and gruesome, Hollywood-quality special effects, *Phantasmagoria: A Puzzle of Flesh* may be the first truly adult-oriented mass-market megahit.

It is, however, still a game. There are puzzles to solve—lots of puzzles. Difficult puzzles. And this is where I come in.

How to Use this Book

This guide is straightforward and easy to use. Note, however, that it does not substitute for the *Phantasmagoria: A Puzzle of Flesh* game manual. As a "strategy guide," this book assumes you've read the manual and are familiar with the *Phantasmagoria* interface. If this isn't the case … well, go away now and read the game documentation. Don't worry, I can wait. Really, I've got all day.

Part One, "*Phantasmagoria*: An Annotated Walkthrough," provides a detailed, step-by-step solution path through the game. The walkthrough is divided into five chapters, one for each of the game's five bloody, murderous days. Use the Table of Contents to find the location or puzzle stumping you, then turn to that section to find the answers you seek.

What does "annotated" mean? In this case, it means you get more than just quick, mindless solutions. You get explanations of plot and/or puzzle logic, you get background information, and you even get a few inside notes on the game design. This short sample illustrates how an annotated walkthrough works:

NAME OF LOCATION/PUZZLE

Sometimes locations or puzzles need a setup or description. In this walkthrough, a few short sentences usually introduce each new venue in the game.

♦ Then comes a list of "action bullet points."

♦ These are tasks you must complete to win the game.

♦ Or, in some cases, a bullet point notes an optional, fun thing to try.

♦ In any case, you can skip all the annotation and simply refer to the action bullet points, if you want.

But sometimes, gamers want more than just answers. They want explanations. You'll find background information, author commentary, discussion of plot or puzzle logic, and other incidental material in paragraphs like this between the action bullet points.

♦ More action bullet points follow.

♦ Soon you win the game.

♦ And after you finish *Phantasmagoria: A Puzzle of Flesh*, you'll never sleep the same.

Part Two, "A Conversation with Lorelei Shannon," introduces you to the creator of *Phantasmagoria: A Puzzle of Flesh*. This interview took place via telephone in November of 1996, just days before the game "went gold"—industry slang for pressing gold master disks, meaning the software code is final and ready for mass replication. I think you'll find Ms. Shannon's perspective on the game and its origins fascnating.

An Annotated Walkthrough

Chapter

Chapter
Chapter
Chapter

Chapter 1

Welcome to the official, annotated walkthrough for the Official Computer Game of the Christian Coalition. (Just kidding, Pat.) If you've played *Phantasmagoria: A Puzzle of Flesh* beyond Chapter 1, you know this is an entirely adult experience—graphic, violent, kinky, horrifying, and sexually explicit. So take that "Parents Advisory" sticker on the game box seriously: This game is not for chidren or the faint of heart.

The game opens with a disturbing, near-psychedelic sequence in a mental hospital. A young man—our star, it turns out—is in the violent throes of what his doctor calls "a psychotic episode" and is rushed to a therapy room for electroshock treatment. The nightmarish scene fades, and we see Curtis Craig awaken in his bed. It's one year later. After Curtis rises to dress for work, the game begins in the bedroom of his apartment.

CURTIS CRAIG'S APARTMENT

Figure 1-1. **MEET CURTIS CRAIG.** Nice guy, nice place. Is everything as it seems?

Bedroom

♦ Click on the dresser mirror. Curtis admires the purple bags under his eyes.

♦ Go right.

♦ Click on the nightstand next to the bed for a closer view.

♦ Open the nightstand drawer.

Chapter One

Figure 1-2. TOTAL GUY DRAWER.
Grab the candy, photo, and screwdriver.
Leave the condom—it's more convenient where it is.

♦ Take the screwdriver.

♦ Take the granola bar.

♦ Take the photograph of parents.

♦ Exit the close-up.

♦ Go left.

♦ Veer left into the living room.

Living Room

♦ Click on the photo on the coffee table for a closer view.

♦ Take the photo. Obviously, it was snapped at a Christmas party.

Figure 1-3. YULE TIED. Ah, the bonds of friendship. Does the Christmas Spirit talk in multiple tongues?

♦ Go left.

♦ Click on the rat cage in the corner. Watch Curtis interact with his pet rat, Blob.

♦ Come forward.

♦ Click on the bookshelf. Find out what kind of books Curtis reads—*Childhood of Pain, The House Next Door, Murder Beach,* and so on.

♦ Click on the small picture hanging left of the bookshelf for a closer view.

Chapter One

Easter egg! Say hello to Sierra's *Phantasmagoria* design team.

Figure 1-4. **THE WHOLE SICK CREW.** You want accountability?
Here it is...the delightfully twisted team who brought you
Phantasmagoria: A Puzzle of Flesh.

♦ Exit the photo close-up.

♦ Go left.

♦ Veer left down the hallway to the front door.

Front Hall

♦ Click on the drop basket on the door. Curtis picks up his mail and ends up facing away from the door.

Figure 1-5. MAIL CHECK. Click on the door's drop basket to retrieve today's mail.

♦ Veer right to return to the living room.

Living Room

♦ Take today's mail from inventory.

♦ Click the mail on Curtis.

Curtis automatically flops onto the couch, sorting his mail. When he's done, a sexy postcard appears in your inventory. So what are you waiting for?

Chapter One

♦ In inventory, examine the sexy postcard.

♦ Click on the magnifying class for a closer view.

♦ Read the steamy note from an anonymous admirer.

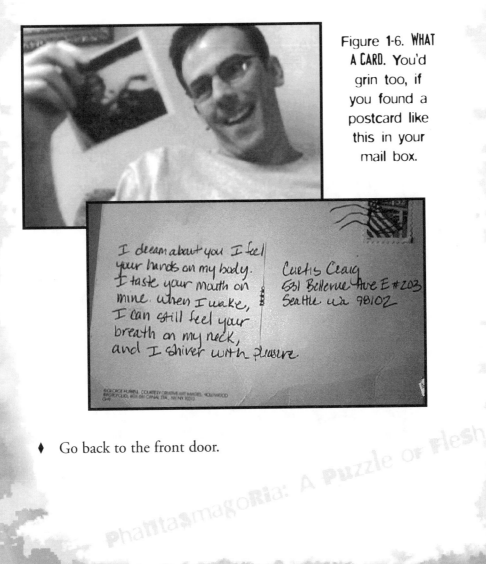

Figure 1-6. **WHAT A CARD.** You'd grin too, if you found a postcard like this in your mail box.

♦ Go back to the front door.

Front Hall

♦ Click on the front door. Oh man. No wallet.

♦ Go back into the living room.

Living Room

♦ Click on the couch. Curtis looks underneath, finds his wallet, but can't reach it.

♦ Go left.

♦ Click on the rat cage. Curtis extracts Blob, who now appears in your inventory.

Figure 1-7.
BLOB JOB. Curtis finds his wallet under the couch.
Blob will retrieve it, but she needs a bit of coaxing—and you know how rats just love granola bars.

- ♦ Go right.

- ♦ Use Blob on the couch. Curtis puts Blob under the couch and orders her to retrieve the wallet.

- ♦ Take the granola bar from inventory.

- ♦ Click the granola bar on the couch. Curtis uses the bar to lure Blob (with wallet).

- ♦ Go back to the front hall.

Front Hall

- ♦ Click on the front door.

Again, Curtis tries to exit…but he remembers Blob, who sits on his shoulder. As Curtis turns to take Blob back to her cage, he makes an interesting remark: "You can't go with me. Bob's the only rat allowed at WynTech." Who's Bob? Let's go find out.

- ♦ On the map screen, travel to WynTech.

Figure 1-8. TRAVEL MAP. So easy to use, I'm almost embarrassed to include a screen shot. Just click on the destination you desire.

WynTech Industries

Main Hallway

Curtis arrives in the main hallway of WynTech Industries, a small pharmaceutical firm in Seattle, Washington. He's a technical writer, a thankless job if ever there was one. His rat-hole, I mean, cubicle, is in the main office area behind the first door on the left. That door is locked, and requires an electronic card key for access. The door on the right side of the main hallway is unlocked, however.

◆ Open the door on the right to enter the WynTech Network Room.

Network Room

◆ Veer right for a closer view of the boxes in the corner of the room.

◆ Click on boxes to move them and reveal an old monitor.

◆ Click on the monitor to move it and reveal a small door.

Figure 1-9. **NETWORKING.** Hey, what's behind all those boxes? Aha! A small, locked door. Must be important, or it wouldn't be in the game.

♦ Try to open the door. It's locked.

♦ Click on the keyhole. Curtis wonders, *Why is this door locked?*

♦ Try the screwdriver on the door. It doesn't work.

♦ Move back from the door. Curtis replaces the old monitor and the boxes.

♦ Exit the Network Room to the hallway.

Main Hallway

♦ In inventory, examine the wallet.

♦ In the close-up, click on the wallet to open it and remove the WynTech card key.

♦ Use the WynTech card key on the electronic key sensor, the device with the glowing red light at far left. Curtis unlocks the door and enters the main office area.

Figure 1-10. KEY DISCOVERY. To enter Wyntech's main office area, take Curtis's card key from his wallet and use it on the key sensor.

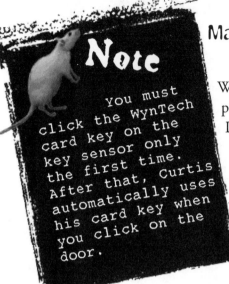

Note

You must click the WynTech card key on the key sensor only the first time. After that, Curtis automatically uses his card key when you click on the door.

Main Office Area

Welcome to WynTech. This area is part of the company's Research and Development unit. Here, Curtis helps produce the unreadable documentation that accompanies most pharmaceutical products. Only seven people work in this area, including WynTech's VP of Research and Development.

♦ Click on the water cooler. Curtis gets a drink.

♦ Go right.

♦ Click on the closed door just down the hallway to the left.

Figure 1-11. VP OF R & D. That door at the far left leads into the office of Paul Allen Warner, one of Curtis's favorite people.

Phantasmagoria: A Puzzle of Flesh

Chapter One

This is the office of Paul Allen Warner, the main-office mucky-muck. Listen to Curtis reveal deep feelings about his illustrious leader: "The less I see of Paul Allen Warner, the happier I'll be."

♦ Veer right to face two cubicle entrances.

♦ Veer left to enter Tom Ravell's cubicle.

Tom Ravell's Cubicle

♦ Click on Tom to talk to him. Curtis reports the completion of one job (the "Venimen documentation") and Tom assigns him another project.

♦ Click the wallet on Tom. Curtis apologizes for being late.

Figure 1-12. TOM RAVELL. He's the unit supervisor, and he seems like a pretty doggone nice guy.

- Click the WynTech card key on Tom. Curtis asks about his security clearance.

- Move back to exit the cubicle.

- Veer right to enter Jocilyn Rowan's cubicle.

Jocilyn Rowan's Cubicle

- Click on Jocilyn. Hmmm. Looks like a "relationship" of some sort.

- Click on Jocilyn again. Curtis makes a date to meet her at the Dreaming Tree after work.

Figure 1-13. MOUTH TO MOUTH. She's breathing! Thank God Curtis got there in time to resuscitate the poor girl.

Chapter One

♦ Use the photograph of parents on Jocilyn. Curtis doesn't seem too happy about his resemblance to his mother. Why?

♦ Use the Christmas party photo on Jocilyn.

♦ Use the sexy postcard on Jocilyn. Oops!

♦ Move back to exit the cubicle.

♦ Go right to return to the hall.

Main Office Area

♦ Veer right to face two more cubicle entrances.

♦ Veer right again to enter Bob Arnold's cubicle.

Bob Arnold's Cubicle

♦ Talk to Bob. What a pleasant guy! Notice his pet name for Curtis: "Ratboy."

♦ Click on Bob again. Curtis makes a singular point.

Figure 1-14. **BOB ARNOLD.** Man, what a total Bob he is.

♦ Move back to exit into the hallway.

♦ Veer left to enter Therese Banning's cubicle.

Therese Banning's Cubicle

♦ Talk to Therese. Playful, isn't she?

♦ Use the sexy postcard on Therese. Suddenly, the plot thickens.

Figure 1-15.
THERESE BANNING,
All-American Girl.
Therese lets you
in on a little
secret. The sexy
postcard's
from her.

- Move back to exit into the hallway.

- Go left to face two more cubicle entrances.

- Veer left to enter Curtis's own cubicle.

Curtis Craig's Cubicle

- Click on the chair to sit down.

Figure 1-16. **A ROOM WITH NO VIEW.** Here's where Curtis slaves away for old man Warner and WynTech.

Enter Trevor Barnes, company clown and Curtis's good friend. After some amusing repartee, Trevor goes to his cubicle next door, empty until now.

♦ Exit Curtis' cubicle.

♦ Veer right into Trevor's cubicle.

Note

This may not seem like the most logical move at this point. But visiting Trevor before starting work lets you see Curtis interact with him, and develops their friendship.

Trevor Barnes' Cubicle

♦ Click on Trevor to talk to him. He invites Curtis to go "clubbing" tonight.

♦ Use the Christmas party photo on Trevor.

♦ Use the sexy postcard on Trevor.

Figure **1-17. TREVOR BARNES.** Meet Curtis's best friend
and confidante.

♦ Use the WynTech card key on Trevor.

♦ Use the photograph of parents on Trevor. Boy, Curtis is awfully
touchy about his mother, isn't he?

♦ Return to Curtis's cubicle.

Curtis Craig's Cubicle

♦ Sit in the chair for a view of the desktop area.

♦ Click on the photo of Blob at left. She is darned pretty, isn't she?

♦ Click on the notepad just left of the keyboard. You see a list of
WynTech phone extensions.

Note

In the phone list, "PAW" is Paul Allen Warner, of course.

TREVOR BARNES	
ME	6125
JOCELYN	6100
TOM	6992
THERESE	6120
BOB	3058
PAW	6114
	6996

Figure 1-18. **PHONE LIST.** Here's a list of extensions for the main office area. **Click** on the phone and use the number pad to call people.

♦ Click on the phone to get a close-up of the number pad.

♦ Dial Jocilyn's extension: 6992.

♦ After Jocilyn hangs up, call her back. Curtis makes an "obscene" call.

Chapter One

♦ Dial Trevor's extension: 6125. Prepare for a classic Crisco reference.

♦ Dial Tom's extension: 6120. Curtis leaves a message.

♦ Dial Therese's extension: 3038.

♦ Dial Bob's extension: 6114. Curtis can't bring himself to talk to (as he so delicately puts it) the "king of the assholes."

♦ Dial PAW's (Paul Allen Warner's) extension: 6996.

♦ For fun, dial extension 6100…Curtis Craig's own number.

♦ Click on the computer. You see the computer's System Login screen.

♦ Enter the password "BLOB."

♦ Press the LOG IN button.

What the hell was that? Something punched Curtis. Did you see a fist? I didn't. What's going on? There's blood on the keyboard. Did someone say, "Freak?" (Hey, Curtis—meet the Hecatomb.)

Figure 1-19. PUNCHING BAG. Something unseen takes a shot at poor Curtis, knocking off his glasses.
Let the phantasmagoria begin!

- Pick up the phone and call Trevor: 6125.

- Dial Curtis's own extension again: 6100. Yikes! Things are getting weird.

- Exit and go to Trevor's cubicle.

Trevor Barnes' Cubicle

- Talk to Trevor. Hey ... do you really think a *virus* slugged Curtis?

- Exit and cross the hall to Therese's cubicle.

Therese Banning's Cubicle

- Talk to Therese about "things in the world we cannot see."

- Exit and return to Curtis's cubicle.

Curtis Craig's Cubicle

- Click on the chair. Curtis sits ... warily.

- Click on the computer for a closer view.

- Under "Available File Subsystems," open the "CurtisC" folder.

- Under "Available Files," open the "Venimen–Sagawa" file.

Figure 1-20.
NON-DROWSY FORMULA.
You'd be punchy,
too, if you had to
write Venimen
documentation
all day.

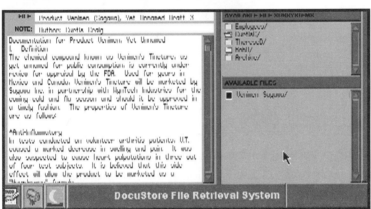

Read Curtis's documentation for a new product, a chemical compound known as Venimen's Tincture. Note that WynTech seems entirely willing to ignore or create excuses for such minor side effects as nosebleeds, heart palpitations, mild hallucinations "involving insects," and nickel-sized purple lesions on the midsection and lower back. Hmmm.

An Annotated Walkthrough

♦ Try to open the "Archive" folder. Note that it is a Secure System protected by a password—that you don't have yet.

♦ Open the "ThereseB" folder.

♦ Open the "Tincture" file. Note that Therese is compiling a list of research reports on Venimen's Tincture.

♦ Open the "BobA" folder.

♦ Open the "Venimen" file. Bob is compiling foreign documentation on Venimen from Canada, Albania, and Mexico.

♦ Open the "Employees" folder.

♦ Read all of the employee files.

You learn a few interesting things from these employee files. Bob Arnold is a technical writer, too, and he's nine years older than Curtis. Perhaps that explains his competitive attitude. Therese Banning, born in 1964, is five years older than Curtis—a woman of experience, perhaps? Tom Ravell is the Unit Supervisor—Curtis's immediate boss. Jocilyn Rowan handles Purchasing at WynTech. As noted earlier, Paul Allen Warner is VP of Research and Development.

♦ Click on the e-mail icon (the mailbox) at lower left.

♦ Read and answer all of Curtis's mail.

It doesn't matter which replies you send to Trevor's jokes or Jocilyn's mushy note. The "Dreams" e-mail from "Fantasy" resembles the note on the sexy postcard. Could it be Therese again? (Or could it be … *Satan?*) Warner's message to all employees reaffirms the sacred nature of restricted areas, and the Legal Department revels it screwed yet another consumer. (Note the brilliant product name—Slimoril!)

Note

If you wait a couple of minutes (or come back to your mailbox later) you find prompt replies from Trevor and Jocilyn.

♦ Click on the document icon—the leftmost icon at the bottom of the screen.

♦ Open the "Venimen–Sagawa" file again.

♦ Click on the document window.

♦ Click on the document window again.

♦ Third clock causes computer to fritz out.

The monitor fritzes out. As Curtis fools with the cables, an unsettling vision suddenly appears on the monitor: It's his mother, sweeping and babbling incoherently. Two large men haul her away.

Figure 1-21. PC BITES. Let this be fair warning to you. See what happens when you mess around with computer cords?

- ♦ Click on the monitor again. The horror continues for poor Curtis.

- ♦ When the vision is over, pick up the phone and call Trevor: 6125.

- ♦ Exit the cubicle.

- ♦ Go to Trevor's cubicle.

Trevor Barnes' Cubicle

♦ Talk to Trevor. He suggests a quick break, and the scene changes to the Dreaming Tree.

THE DREAMING TREE

♦ Click on the waiter, Max, to talk to him.

♦ Talk to Trevor three times.

Figure 1-22. **THE DREAMING TREE.** Trevor drags Curtis from work to a favorite lunch hangout for a heart-to-heart. Click on Trev three times to hear the whole story.

After some coaxing, Curtis unloads the news of his recent travails on his best buddy. Aside from the hallucinations, he's just recently recalled his mother's suicide. Trevor's good ear and humor both help, and the two head back to WynTech.

WynTech Industries

Main Hallway

♦ Open the door on the right to enter the Network Room.

Network Room

♦ Watch the near-seduction scene with Therese.

♦ Exit and return to the main office area.

Figure 1-23.
ON THE PROWL.
Therese finally gets Curtis where she wants him—alone in the Network Room.

Chapter One

Main Office Area

For another brush with Therese, try a drink from the water cooler. (Note her prophetic comment: "There's more to you than meets the eye.") Looks like things are getting out of hand ... so to speak. Better nip this in the bud.

♦ Go to Therese's cubicle.

Therese Banning's Cubicle

♦ Talk to Therese. This gal's got a thing about "flesh," doesn't she?

♦ Go to Curtis's cubicle.

Curtis Craig's Cubicle

♦ Sit in the chair.

♦ Click on the monitor.

♦ Open the "CurtisC" folder.

♦ Open the "Venimen–Sagawa" file.

Instead of a document, up pops a puzzle of some sort. Letters cycle in six squares. Man, who would do a thing like that to a nice guy like Curtis?

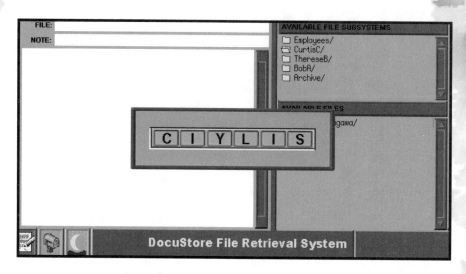

Figure 1-24. **ALPHA-PUZZLE**. Somebody blocked access to the Venimen file. Curtis suspects Bob. What six-letter code word might Bob find amusing?

♦ Exit the computer interface.

♦ Go to Bob's cubicle.

Bob Arnold's Cubicle

♦ Talk to Bob. He's stunned by your "incompetence."

♦ Go to Trevor's cubicle.

Trevor Barnes' Cubicle

♦ Talk to Trevor. More talk of the promotion. Note Curtis's flip comment: "Think anybody'd mind if I killed him?"

♦ Go back to Curtis's cubicle.

Curtis Craig's Cubicle

♦ Sit in the chair.

♦ Click on the monitor.

♦ Open the "Venimen–Sagawa" file to retrieve the puzzle.

Note that when you click on any of the squares, the letters stop cycling and the current letter freezes in place. You can click on frozen letters to restart the cycling.

Figure 1-25. PUZZLE SOLUTION

An Annotated Walkthrough

- Click on the letter squares to form the word "RATBOY." Hey, wasn't that Bob's nickname for Curtis?

- Exit the computer interface.

- Exit the cubicle to the hallway.

- Go to Bob's cubicle. Let's have a few words with him, shall we?

Bob Arnold's Cubicle

- Talk to Bob. Curtis gets tough … sort of.

- Exit the cubicle into the hallway.

- Turn right. Say, did Mr. Warner leave his door ajar?

- Click on Paul Allen Warner's door.

Paul Allen Warner's Office

- Go left.

- Examine the plaque on the wall at far left: "Carpe Diem." Remember that.

Figure 1-26. INNER SANCTUM. Looks like Paul Allen Warner knows how to get a head in the world. Check out that plaque on the wall next to the antelope.

♦ Click on the desktop for a better view.

♦ Click on the family portrait.

Do you hear something? Sounds like an argument. Somebody says, "You've got to stop it, or I will." Then a familiar voice answers, "I'll kill you, you son of a bitch." And the audio portion of our broadcast concludes with a dull, heavy thud.

♦ Open the desk drawer.

Oops! Caught red-handed. Paul Allen Warner manages to be pompous and creepy at the same time. After the embarrassment, Curtis ends up back in the hallway.

Figure 1-27. **LAME EXCUSE AWARD.** *Word* 8 manual—yeah, right. You think he bought it?

♦ Go back to Curtis's cubicle.

Curtis Craig's Cubicle

♦ Sit in the chair.

♦ Open the "Venimen–Sagawa" file (if it's not already open).

♦ Click on the document … and watch the workday end.

♦ Exit the cubicle.

♦ Exit into the main hallway.

♦ Enter the Network Room.

Network Room

Holy snakes, Batman! Watch the cables come alive. Then end up back outside the room.

Figure 1-28. **WIRED FOR HORROR.** See what happens when you deregulate the cable industry?

♦ Exit Wyntech. Remember, Curtis has a date.

♦ On the map, travel to the Dreaming Tree.

THE DREAMING TREE

♦ Talk to Jocilyn. Gee, what a sweet gal!

♦ Talk to Max the waiter.

♦ Talk to Jocilyn twice more.

An Annotated Walkthrough

After the third click on Jocilyn, Curtis gets a really pleasant visitation from the Hecatomb. Who is this guy? Why is he in the bushes? What's he got stuck in his throat?

Figure 1-29. **BUSH MAN.** Nothing like a bloody visitation to ruin a perfectly good date.

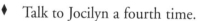

♦ Talk to Jocilyn a fourth time.

♦ Take the wallet from inventory.

♦ Click the wallet on the check on the table to pay the tab.

Figure 1-30. **FLASH CARD.** Curtis finds Dr. Harburg's card in his wallet, triggering a flashback to his dismissal from the hospital.

Chapter One

When Curtis pulls out his wallet, a business card falls out. Looking at it triggers a brief flashback: Curtis receives a card from a man outside a hospital. After it fades, Curtis pays the tab…and the lovebirds head back to Curtis's apartment

CURTIS CRAIG'S APARTMENT

Living Room

Curtis and Jocilyn enter and sit on the couch. The card that fell from Curtis's wallet is now in your inventory. It's the business card for a psychiatrist named Dr. Rikki Harburg.

Figure 1-31. DR. HARBURG'S CARD. Given today's events, maybe Curtis should give the doc a buzz.

♦ Click on Jocilyn to trigger the end-of-chapter movie. (Parents, be warned: In the "More Intense" version of the game, it's steamy and sexually explicit.)

Figure 1-32. POSTCOITAL BLUES. Curtis and Jocilyn had a pretty good night … but mornings after can be hell.

An Annotated Walkthrough

Chapter

Chapter

Chapter

Chapter

Chapter 2

After another ghoulish nightmare, Curtis jolts awake, alone in bed. Apparently, Jocilyn woke early and hustled home to prep herself for work. Cut to Curtis's WynTech cubicle, where Bob Arnold is about to sabotage our hero's hard drive—but suddenly hears a menacing voice behind him. Cut back to the Curtis in his bedroom. He wipes his face at his dresser mirror.

Notice the towel as he tosses it down.

Is that blood?

Front Hall

♦ Go into the front hall.

CURTIS CRAIG'S APARTMENT

Front Hall

♦ Click on the drop box to get the mail.

♦ Go into the living room.

Living Room

♦ Click today's mail on Curtis. He sorts the mail.

♦ Examine what your inventory calls a "greeting card." (Ha!) The card is signed "T." —Therese, no doubt.

 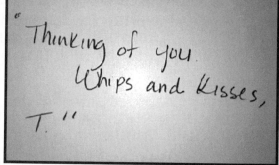

Figure 2-1. FUNNY GAG. This greeting card from Therese shows a lot of restraint.

Chapter Two

♦ Click Dr. Harburg's business card on the phone. Curtis makes an appointment.

Figure 2-2. **APPOINTMENT.** Be sure to call Doc Harburg and set up an appointment for after work.

Note

Making this phone call adds the office of "Doc Harburg" to your travel map.

♦ Go left.

♦ Click on the rat cage. Curtis compliments Miss Blob.

♦ Travel to WynTech.

WynTech Industries

Main Hallway

Curtis arrives to see a cop talking to his fellow employees in the hallway. Everybody looks pretty upset. Whoa. What's up?

Figure 2-3. CRIME SCENE. Something's terribly amiss at WynTech Industries. Better ask what's going on.

♦ Talk to Jocilyn. Way to be supportive, Curtis!

♦ Talk to Trevor. Doesn't look good, whatever it is.

Chapter Two

Figure 2-4. PRE-HURL. Hang on, Trev.
The bathroom's just down the hall.

♦ Talk to Therese. Nobody's talking much, are they?

♦ Click on the main office door. The cop turns Curtis away from what he calls an "active crime scene."

♦ Click on the door next to the main office door. It's unlocked, and it leads into Paul Allen Warner's office.

PAUL ALLEN WARNER'S OFFICE

Curtis slips quietly into the office, where another cop talks on the phone.

♦ For fun, just hang in the office and listen to the cop repeat the same replies until you go insane. (OK, maybe not.)

♦ Click on the Post-it Note on the floor just behind Curtis.

♦ Take the Post-it Note.

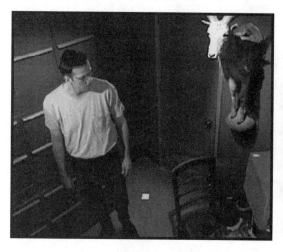

Figure 2-5. **BACK DOOR MAN.** Pretty stealthy move, slipping behind that cop. But don't miss that Post-it Note by Curtis's feet. Three odd words ... what do they mean?

♦ Exit through the door just behind Curtis; it leads into the main office area.

MAIN OFFICE AREA

Get ready for some phantasmagoria of the first order. As Curtis enters the crime scene, watch the grisly flashbacks of Bob's murder (Just a note: there is a "less" intense version of this movie). Some sick fellow stakes Bob to the cubicle wall with X-Acto knives, staples his mouth shut, then guts him with a box cutter. After Curtis stumbles into his cubicle and sees the mutilated Bob, Detective Allie Powell leads him away and begins to question him.

Chapter Two

Figure 2-6. **CRIME SCENE.** Curtis manages to pick his way through cops and coroners to his cubicle before Detective Allie Powell stops him.

♦ Click on Detective Powell to ask her a question. Curtis learns about the weapons used—the X-Acto knives, staple gun, and box cutter.

♦ Wait until Detective Powell asks about Bob.

At this point, Curtis notices something very peculiar. Looks like someone is dragging Bob's body bag back into Curtis's cubicle. I don't see any coroners around. Do you?

♦ During the next lull in the interrogation, click on the entrance to Curtis's cubicle (left side of the aisle). And brace yourself.

Watch the Hecatomb harass Curtis, chew bloody entrails, etc. He looks an awful lot like Curtis, doesn't he? And such a refined sense of humor! Note his comment: "Just a witness to your crimes."

Note

By the way, my edition of Webster's New Collegiate Dictionary defines "hecatomb" as "the sacrifice or slaughter of many victims." Just so you know what you're in for.

♦ Click again on the entrance to Curtis's cubicle for a final shocker from the Hecatomb.

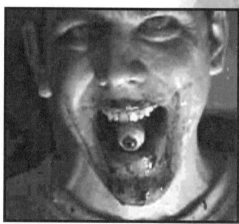

Figure 2-7. BOB IN DRAG. Who's dragging Bob? Oh, it's the Hecatomb. Better keep an eye on that fellow.

Chapter Two

Detective Powell lets Curtis go, and Tom calls an impromptu employee meeting. The scene automatically shifts to the Dreaming Tree.

THE DREAMING TREE

After Tom leaves for drinks and a shaken Trevor begs off for the day, Curtis is left with Jocilyn and Therese.

Figure 2-8. **THE WOMEN OF WYNTECH.** Jocilyn and Therese hunker with Curtis at the Dreaming Tree for drinks, grieving, and dark jokes about the Bad Karma Fairy.

♦ Talk to Jocilyn twice. Curtis's cold, odd sense of humor drives her right out the door.

♦ Talk to Therese three times. She makes a date for 7 p.m. at a club called the Borderline, then leaves.

Note

This adds the Borderline to your travel map.

Curtis automatically goes back to his apartment.

Living Room

♦ Click on Blob's cage. Thanks for the vote of confidence, rat girl.

♦ Click on the bookcase. Man, I hate vivisection flashbacks.

Figure 2-9. WHAT'S UP, DOC? Is that a scalpel? Who's that guy? What's he doing in your bookshelf?

- Go into the bedroom.

Bedroom

- Click on the mirror. Curtis hears an accusatory voice and spins around to see—nothing.

- Travel back to WynTech.

WynTech Industries

Main Hallway

- Click on Paul Allen Warner's door. Listen to business as usual. What a cold-hearted bastard!

- Enter the main office area.

Main Office Area

Curtis automatically goes to his cubicle, and an angry Detective Powell kicks him out.

- Re-enter the main office area.

- Enter Tom's empty cubicle.

Tom Ravell's Cubicle

♦ Pick up Tom's phone.

♦ Click on Paul Allen Warner's extension on the phone list. Curtis tricks Warner into leaving his office.

Figure 2-10. **PHONE FRAUD.** Ah, the old "meet-me-in-the-fourth-floor-conference-room" ruse. Use Tom's phone to lure Warner out of his office. (The phone's just to the right of his chair.)

♦ Go into Paul Allen Warner's office.

Chapter Two

Paul Allen Warner's Office

♦ Click on the desktop for a closer view.

♦ Click on the computer.

♦ Read the onscreen document—an address to the WynTech Board of Directors.

Interdimensionality? Wow. This Threshold project with its "flux controls" sounds pretty bizarre. Note the reference to a 30-year hiatus.

♦ Exit the computer close-up.

♦ Click on the family portrait for a scary vision. Blood!

♦ Open the desk drawer.

Figure 2-11. ANOTHER KEY DISCOVERY. This time Curtis manages to get into Warner's drawers to grab the old man's key.

PhaNtaSmagoRia: A PuZzle oF FleSh

- Take the key.

- Exit the drawer close-up.

Busted again! Warner makes some cryptic references to Curtis's father. After the confrontation, Curtis automatically exits the room into the main office area.

- Go into Bob's cubicle.

Bob Arnold's Cubicle

- Click on Bob's desk just beneath his keyboard.

- In the close-up of the carpet, take the button.

- Exit the close-up.

Figure 2-12.
CONVERSATION PIECE.
Look for that hot spot just under Bob's desk, then nab the button on the floor. You need it later to initiate discussion of Bob's murder.

Phantasmagoria: A Puzzle of Flesh

♦ Exit the main office area.

♦ Enter the Network Room.

Network Room

♦ Veer right to the back corner.

♦ Move the stack of boxes.

♦ Move the monitor to reveal the small door.

♦ Use Warner's key on the lock. Curtis enters a hidden storage room.

Figure 2-13. **TOOLS OF THE TRADE.** Curtis unlocks a hidden storage room. He finds a sledgehammer smeared with—red paint?

Hidden Storage Room

♦ Click on the file cabinet (bottom of screen) to open it.

♦ Take the toolbox from the file drawer.

♦ Click on the toolbox to trigger a strobe-like hallucination. (Not recommended for claustrophobic people.)

♦ When the vision ends, exit the storage room.

♦ Travel to Curtis's apartment.

CURTIS CRAIG'S APARTMENT

Front Hall

♦ Veer right into the living room.

Living Room

♦ Take the toolbox from inventory.

♦ Click the toolbox on Curtis to open it.

Figure 2-14. **BOLTED BOXTOP.**
The top tray of the toolbox
holds a file labeled
"Threshold" and a
small lacy dress.

But Curtis can't see
what's beneath the
tray—it's bolted in.

♦ Take the lacy dress. It seems to trigger an unpleasant memory for
Curtis. (A piece of the lace appears in your inventory.)

♦ Take the Threshold file folder.

♦ In inventory, examine the Threshold file and read the letter from
Warner.

♦ Click on the top tray in the toolbox.

Curtis tries to pull out the tray, but discovers it's bolted in. No time
to fool with it now; Curtis has a doctor's appointment, remember?

♦ Try screwdriver on toolbox. Still doesn't open.

♦ Click file folder on Curtis to read document contained in folder.

♦ Travel to Dr. Harburg's office.

Dr. Harburg's Office

Welcome to the tasteful, sunny office of Dr. Rikki Harburg. Do you like the decor? Let's talk about it, shall we?

♦ After Curtis meets Dr. Harburg, click on her once.

Figure 2-15.
DR. RIKKI HARBURG.
The doc looks helpful and concerned, in a professional sort of way. Open your heart (and inventory) to her.

♦ Show Bob's button to Dr. Harburg. Curtis reveals his strange lack of feeling about Bob's bloody demise.

♦ Click on the snowstorm paperweight on Dr. Harburg's desk (just left of her shoulder). For Curtis, it triggers another painful memory of his mother.

Chapter Two

Figure 2-16. **MOMMY'S LITTLE FREAK.** The snowstorm paperweight on Dr. Harburg's desk triggers an awful flashback for poor Curtis.

♦ Show the Christmas party photo to Dr. Harburg. Curtis reveals his attraction to Trevor.

♦ Show the photograph of parents to Dr. Harburg. Note how he recalls his father's death: "Run down by a drunk in an old Plymouth."

♦ Show the Threshold file to Dr. Harburg. Learn that whatever the project is, Curtis's father was "deeply involved."

♦ Show the lace to Dr. Harburg to reveal some more of Curtis's deep secrets.

♦ Show the lace to her again.

Figure 2-17. THE WAY WE WERE. Ah, a boy and his mom. With memories like these, who needs nightmares?

♦ Show the sexy postcard to Dr. Harburg.

♦ Show the bondage greeting card to Dr. Harburg.

♦ Click Dr. Harburg's card on her. Curtis mentions Dr. Marek, the doctor who treated him at the psychiatric hospital.

♦ When the session ends, travel to the Dreaming Tree.

THE DREAMING TREE

♦ Talk to Max twice. Favorite line: When he hears details of Bob's murder, Max surmises that "he must have really pissed somebody off in Shipping".

♦ Click on the table menu twice.

♦ Travel to the Borderline.

Chapter Two

BORDERLINE CLUB

Club Front Door

The Borderline is not the type of establishment you or I frequent. Well, maybe you do. Watch the Egyptian drill team bob past; watch the leathery bouncer toss the woman to the ground; watch the bouncer stop Curtis at the door. What a fun place!

Figure 2-18. THE BORDERLINE. And that guy's the border patrol. Do you have an item that might convince him you know Therese?

♦ Talk to the bouncer.

♦ Show the sexy postcard to the bouncer. No go.

♦ Show the bondage greeting card to the bouncer. He lets you in.

Main Dance Area

Welcome to the Borderline, a real family-values sort of place. Milk and cookies available at the bar.

Figure 2-19. CAPTIVE AUDIENCE. Interesting clientele. Is there a gas leak?

♦ Talk to the patron at the bar. Oops!

♦ Approach the doors on the left.

♦ Click on the bathroom door but you cannot enter. (There is also a "less" intense version of this.)

Figure 2-20. REST ROOM. People don't go in there to rest, though. Not at the Borderline, anyway.

Chapter Two

♦ Move back from the bathroom to see the bar again.

♦ Veer right to the back room door.

♦ Try to go through the door. Curtis gets turned away from what the bouncer calls "the Pit."

♦ Step back from the bouncer.

♦ Turn left to see Therese. Curtis joins her in a booth.

♦ Talk to Therese three times.

Figure 2-21.
BIG COMFY COUCH.
Join Therese for a drink. At this point, ask yourself the same question she asks Curtis: "Do you need a drink ... to cope with the ugly truth?"

After the third click on Therese, a bartender delivers a drink for Curtis. Guess who? Yep—that's Max from the Dreaming Tree.

Figure 2-22. LAST CALL? I've never had a Red Shiny Rubber, but I hear it's sort of like a Shirley Temple with a shot of diesel fuel.

♦ Click on the drink. Curtis knocks it right back.

♦ After the Piercer asks for a navel-piercing volunteer, you can either wait for Therese to "volunteer" Curtis, or click on the Piercer to have Curtis volunteer on his own. (It doesn't matter which; the ensuing action is the same for either choice.)

This triggers a hallucinatory sequence: Curtis is pierced not only by the Piercer's instruments, but also by a very disturbing flashback.

Figure 2-23. **NAVEL ACADEMY.** The Piercer is scary enough without a Mommy Dearest flashback to compound the agony.

The movie concludes with another R-rated interlude—Curtis hauls Therese into the Borderline restroom for some good old-fashioned countertop copulation. (Remember, there is a "less" intense version of this sequence available.) When it's all over, Curtis ends up in bed, contemplating his navel.

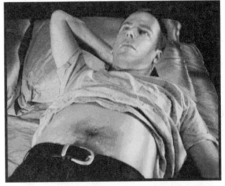

Figure 2-24. **ABS OF STEEL.** This just might be the scariest shot in the whole damn game.

♦ Click on Curtis's pierced navel for a horrible, chapter-ending hallucination and dream.

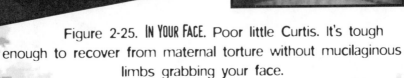

Figure 2-25. **IN YOUR FACE.** Poor little Curtis. It's tough enough to recover from maternal torture without mucilaginous limbs grabbing your face.

Phantasmagoria: A Puzzle of Flesh

An Annotated Walkthrough

Chapter
Chapter
Chapter
Chapter
Chapter 3

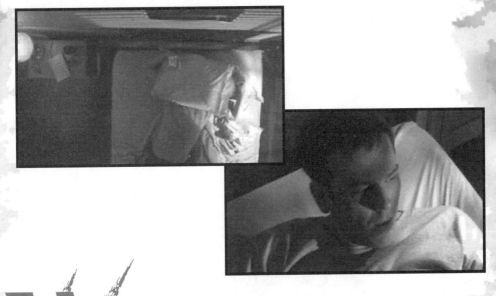

Wrestling with pillows and inner demons, Curtis thrashes awake to face yet another cheery day in sunny Seattle. Chapter 3 action begins in his bedroom.

CURTIS CRAIG'S APARTMENT

Bedroom

♦ Look in the mirror. Aside from a good grimace, not much happens today.

♦ Go into the living room.

Living Room

♦ Click on the phone to answer it. Paul Allen Warner tells Curtis to "get his lazy bones" in to work; Curtis ends up at the front door.

Figure 3-1. **CALL TO ARMS.** Boss Warner could care less about homicide on the premises. Hell, Bob was only a tech writer.

Front Hall

♦ Get the mail from the drop box.

♦ Go into the living room.

Chapter Three

Living Room

♦ Click today's mail on Curtis to sort it.

And welcome to the *Phantasmagoria* Inside Joke Department. Curtis reads a card advertising an upcoming book-signing at a local bookstore. Those of you who played the first *Phantasmagoria* may recognize the author, Adrienne Delaney.

Figure 3-2. COPING WITH LOSS. Famous author Adrienne Delaney is in town for a book-signing. Do you think she'll wear black jeans and an orange T-shirt? (Fans of the original *Phantasmagoria* know what I mean.)

♦ Click on the rat cage to talk to Blob.

♦ Travel to WynTech

WynTech Industries

Main Hallway

♦ Enter the Network Room at right.

Network Room

♦ Veer right to the corner. The small door is plastered over!

♦ Click on the plastered door to hear Curtis state the obvious.

Figure 3-3. PLASTERED. Rats! Curtis really wanted to go back into the hidden storage room and get brutally harassed by monsters again.

♦ Click on the desk.

♦ Take the hammer.

Figure 3-4. **GET HAMMERED.** You never know when a good claw hammer might come in handy.

♦ Exit the Network Room into the main hallway, then go back into the Network Room for an eyefull of the Hecacomb.

♦ Go to the main office area.

Main Office Area

Your entrance triggers an automatic sequence. Detective Powell argues with Paul Allen Warner about tampering with a crime scene. After they retire to Warner's office, Curtis enters his now-sanitized cubicle.

Figure 3-5. **PUBLIC DISAGREEMENT.** Detective Powell isn't too fond of Warner's "little redecorating scheme."

Curtis Craig's Cubicle

♦ Click on the computer.

♦ Under System Login Accounts, click on "CurtisC."

♦ Type Curtis's password ("BLOB"), then click the LOG IN button. Note the new folder titled "Memos."

♦ Watch the folder names for a few moments. See anything unusual?

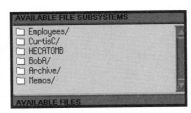

Figure 3-6. **HACKING AROUND.** Log into the WynTech net and
see the messages from the Hecatomb.
He sure is a jolly bastard, isn't he?

The Hecatomb has some fun at Curtis's expense. From now on,
whenever you log in as CurtisC, you'll see file and folder names
change to DIE, LOVEDEATH, USE YOUR TEETH, USURPER,
HECATOMB, EAT THEIR EYES, I AM YOUR DEATH, MON-
STER, CANNIBAL, KILL THEM ALL, BLOOD IS SWEET,
BASTARD, WALLOW IN DEPRAVITY, and other loving messages from your tormentor.

♦ Click on the e-mail mailbox icon.

♦ Read and reply to all of Curtis's e-mail.

Some of it's not too pleasant—in particular, that little note from the
Hecatomb titled "Me" sent out under Curtis's name to all employees. Oh, and that one titled "Your Career" from Curtis's dad. That's
a fun one, too. And don't miss "Hell." It's a dark hoot.

♦ Click on the documents icon.

♦ Open the "CurtisC" folder.

♦ Open the "Alotharia9.doc" file to see Curtis's new project.

♦ Click on the document window to hear how Curtis feels about work today.

♦ Open the "Archive" folder.

♦ Type in the Secure System password.

What? You haven't figured it out yet? OK, here's a hint: Think about your exploration of old man Warner's office. Did any phrase jump out at you? Come on, I'm waiting.

Figure 3-7. **CODE BLOCK.** Nothing's more annoying than people who want privacy. The Archives password is somewhere on Warner's office wall.

♦ Time's up. Type in "CARPE DIEM."

♦ Click the OK button. A file titled "Threshold.doc" appears.

♦ Open the "Threshold.doc" file and read it. Not much info here.

♦ Open the "Memos" folder.

♦ Click on the "Access.doc" file.

Chapter Three

Another password window comes up. In fact, all three files in the "Memos" folder require passwords. What are these passwords? Well, you have them in your inventory right now. Remember the three words on the Post-it Note Curtis found on the floor in Warner's office? (You *did* find it, didn't you?)

Figure 3-8. **PASSWORDS.** These three words will grant access to the files in the "Memos" folder.

♦ The password for the Access.doc file is "INFECTION."

♦ The password for the Energy.doc file is "REVELATION."

♦ The password for the Curtis.doc file is "DESECRATION."

♦ Open and read all three files.

Apparently, something weird is going on down in the basement. And it appears that Curtis is somehow part of the situation, whatever it is. Note the reference to him as "a special employee" in Warner's third note.

♦ Exit the computer.

♦ Pick up the phone and call Trevor: 6125.

♦ Pick up the phone and call Jocilyn: 6992.

- For fun, pick up the phone and call Bob: 6114.

- When the phone rings, answer it. Hi Bob!

- For still more fun, call Therese—3038—then call her again.

- Call Curtis's number: 6100. "Sorry, man, I can't talk now. I'm right in the middle of disemboweling somebody."

Figure 3-10. MORE PHONE FUN. Call Bob, call yourself, call Therese a second time. Ooooo, scary!

- Exit the cubicle.

- Go to Trevor's cubicle.

Chapter Three

Trevor Barnes' Cubicle

♦ Talk to Trevor three times.

♦ Go to Therese's cubicle.

Therese Banning's Cubicle

♦ Talk to Therese.

♦ Click on Therese again. Wow!

Figure 3-11. **GOOD THERESE, BAD THERESE.** Make a couple of visits to Therese's cubicle. She's really happy to see you both times ... but the second time she's just a little bit more insistent.

Therese's parting comment is one of my *Phantasmagoria* favorites: "Think decaf, babe."

♦   Exit Therese's cubicle.

♦   Go to Bob's cubicle.

Bob Arnold's Cubicle

♦   Click on the box to see the hallucination.

Figure 3-12. BOB'S FUN BOX. Look, it's Bob's stuff. He's dead, so he probably won't be needing all those pencils and intestines and things.

♦   Go into Jocilyn's cubicle.

Chapter Three

Jocilyn Rowan's Cubicle

♦ Talk to Jocilyn twice.

Figure 3-13. **YEAH, RIGHT.** When Joss confronts him, Curtis does what any red-blooded man might do in his situation—tells a shameless, bald-faced lie.

♦ Exit Jocilyn's cubicle.

Main Office Area

♦ Click on Paul Allen Warner's door to hear Detective Powell ream the old man for destroying blood evidence.

♦ Go back to Curtis's cubicle. Curtis has another bloody vision.

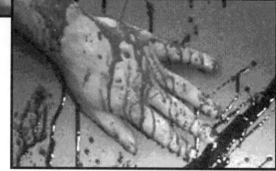

Figure 3-14. OUT, DAMNED SPOT! Next time Curtis reads *Macbeth*, he'll have an entirely new perspective.

♦ Return to Mr. Warner's door. Once again, it's ajar.

♦ Click on Warner's door. Warner and Tom Ravell engage in a furious argument that concludes with a chilling threat.

Figure 3-15. WARNER'S THREAT. "You are a dead man!" Warner's words to Tom Ravell trigger another "episode" for Curtis.

Chapter Three

Warner's words echo deep within Curtis's psyche. He flashes back to a similar scene between Warner and his father. That, in turn, triggers another hallucinatory episode. Curtis finds himself strapped into a chair in a creepy mental hospital.

MENTAL HOSPITAL (HALLUCINATION)

OK, maybe it's a hallucination, but Curtis can't get out of this mess unless he takes action. Your goal: Guide Curtis the hell out of this loony bin.

Figure 3-16. **IT'S ALL MENTAL.** Have you ever wanted to meet the cast of a Fellini movie? Here's your big chance.

♦ Talk to the nurse. *What* health care crisis?

♦ Click on each of the two patients rolling the jingling dog toy.

PhaNtaSmagoRia: A Puzzle of Flesh

Figure 3-17. CUCKOO'S
NEST. The ward nurse
is a real scream. Too
bad the screamer's
not a real nurse.

♦ Click on the patient standing behind the chair.

Here's another of my favorite moments in the game. For some truly
bizarre dark humor, keep clicking on the "hair stylist" standing behind
the bozo-head in the chair. He has an impressive number of responses.

Figure 3-18.
POPPED CULTURE. What do
disco, pizza, Barbie,
Harry Belafonte,
Cheerios, and taco
salad have in
common?
Hell if I know.
Ask this guy.

Chapter Three

- Talk to the woman under the table (right foreground). She tells Curtis, "I saw your guts!" OK, babe.

- Talk to her again. Something's eating her.

- Click on Curtis for a closer view.

- Click on the buckle on his chest. Curtis tries to free himself, but the nurse threatens to sedate him.

Click on the jingling dog toy the two patients push back and forth across the floor in front of Curtis. Curtis uses it to create a diversion.

Figure 3-19.
DIVERSIONARY TACTIC. Kick the doggie ball across the room to divert Nurse Ratchet's attention. Then unbuckle Curtis and run!

Phantasmagoria: A Puzzle of Flesh

- Click on Curtis for another close-up view.

- Click on the buckle.

- Go right. See the hallway?

- Veer right again down the hall to escape.

Curtis makes a break for it—only to be caught by Dr. Marek. After a shockingly unpleasant interlude, Curtis awakens back at WynTech, with various friends and lovers hovering worriedly over him.

Figure 3-20.
BACK TO THE FUTURE.
Curtis? Are you there? It's us ... your fellow WynTech lab rats.

After Curtis revives, Tom Ravell makes a unilateral decision to send everyone home.

- Travel to the Dreaming Tree.

THE DREAMING TREE

- Talk to Trevor four times.

Figure 3-21. BUDDIES. Trevor and Curtis trade deep thoughts
(and stories about bunnies) at the Dreaming Tree.
Did Curtis kill Bob? He's not sure.

The guys share their post-trauma trepidation about Bob's murder;
Trevor recounts a "spud-hits-rabbit" tale; Curtis confesses his homi-
cidal urges toward Bob; then Trevor heads off for a big date with
some guy he met at a Pre-Raphaelite exhibit.

♦ Travel to Curtis's home.

CURTIS CRAIG'S APARTMENT

♦ After you arrive, go into the living room.

Living Room

- Take the toolbox from inventory.

- Click the toolbox on Curtis. He opens it.

- In inventory, examine the hammer for a close-up view.

- *Leave the hammer close-up window open!* In inventory, scroll to the screwdriver and take it.

- Click the screwdriver on the hammer to combine the two tools. (See Figure 3-22.)

Figure 3-22. TOOL COMBO. Combine the hammer and screwdriver; then use them to knock out the tray bolts in the toolbox.

- Click the 'X' in the corner to close the close-up window. The combined tools should be your cursor now.

- Click the hammer/screwdriver combination on the toolbox tray. Curtis uses them to unbolt and remove the top tray.

- Take the letter from the toolbox.

Chapter Three

♦ In inventory, read the letter. Note that you can move the letter up and down to read the whole thing.

♦ To exit the letter, scroll back up to the top and click on the magnifying-glass icon.

♦ Exit the view of the toolbox.

♦ Take the "Letter from Father" from inventory.

♦ Click the letter on Curtis to see him read it.

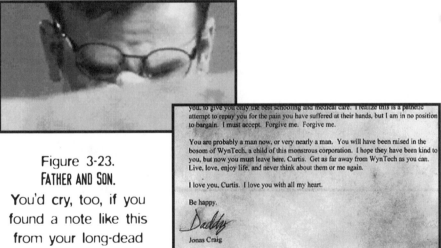

Figure 3-23.
FATHER AND SON.
You'd cry, too, if you found a note like this from your long-dead father, conveying his love from beyond the grave ... and signed "Daddy."

you, to give you only the best schooling and medical care. I realize this is a pathetic attempt to repay you for the pain you have suffered at their hands, but I am in no position to bargain. I must accept. Forgive me. Forgive me.

You are probably a man now, or very nearly a man. You will have been raised in the bosom of WynTech, a child of this monstrous corporation. I hope they have been kind to you, but now you must leave here, Curtis. Get as far away from WynTech as you can. Live, love, enjoy life, and never think about them or me again.

I love you, Curtis. I love you with all my heart.

Be happy,

Daddy
Jonas Craig

♦ Click on Blob's cage, freak boy.

♦ Click on the bookshelf.

♦ Go into the bedroom.

Bedroom

♦ Look in the mirror.

Figure 3-24.
RED-EYE EXPRESS.
Curtis really
ought to have
something done
about that
mirror.

♦ Travel to Dr. Harburg's office.

DR. HARBURG'S OFFICE

♦ Click on Dr. Harburg to talk to her. She wants "groundwork."
Fair enough.

♦ Show Dr. Harburg the photograph of parents.

Figure 3-25. **ANOTHER BAD HAIR DAY.** Remembering Dad triggers more painful memories of Mom.

♦ Show Dr. Harburg the Christmas party photo.

♦ Show Dr. Harburg the sexy postcard.

♦ Show Dr. Harburg the bondage greeting card.

♦ Show Dr. Harburg the Threshold file.

♦ Show Dr. Harburg the letter from father.

♦ Show Dr. Harburg the letter from father again.

An Annotated Walkthrough

Figure 3-26.
MINING TRUTH. Curtis spills his guts (figuratively) about his fear of the Threshold project and his father's suspicious death.

♦ Show Dr. Harburg the lace. In the flashback, note the odd question asked by Curtis's mother: "What's under that crawly, slimy skin of yours?"

♦ Finally, show Dr. Harburg the button from Bob's cubicle. Hey, Curtis … certain speculations are best left unexpressed.

After the session ends, listen to Dr. Harburg's new diagnosis of Curtis. Doesn't sound good, does it?

Figure 3-27. DOC'S DIAGNOSIS. Delusional, possibly paranoid ... with the potential for violence. Fortunately, that doesn't preclude a run for the U.S. Senate!

♦ Travel to the Borderline.

BORDERLINE CLUB

♦ After Curtis enters the club, talk to the patron at the bar.

♦ Try to enter the back room (the Pit) again.

♦ Travel to Curtis's apartment.

CURTIS CRAIG'S APARTMENT

Uh-oh. The door's ajar. Curtis enters cautiously. (By the way, note his apartment number—13.) Therese waits inside. She's indeed a woman of many talents.

Figure 3-28.
WHO'S THERE? Maybe somebody ate your porridge, sat in your chair, and waits you-know-where.

Living Room

♦ Talk to Therese. This triggers a transition to the bedroom.

Bedroom

♦ Click on Therese twice.

Figure 3-29.
HARNESS YOUR ENERGY. Curtis always wanted to hang around with Therese. But who invited that pasty white guy?

Chapter Three

Hey, here's a computer game first: Hero suspended from ceiling in bondage harness, about to be eaten alive by his father. Cool! And then we cut to WynTech, where Tom Ravell composes a letter condemning the actions of Paul Allen Warner. Unfortunately, the note also condemns Tom. To death.

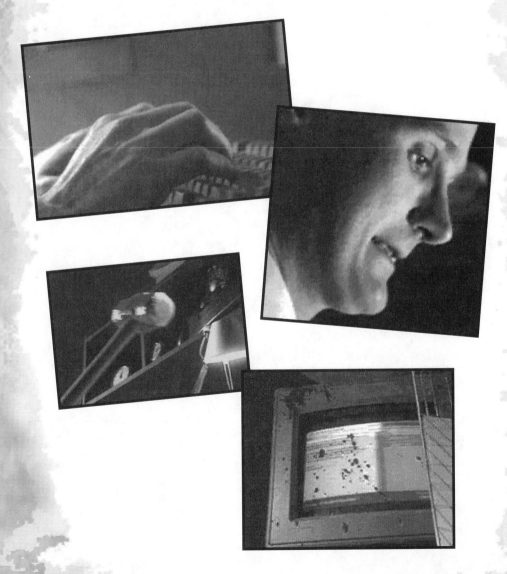

An Annotated Walkthrough

Chapter
Chapter
Chapter
Chapter
Chapter 4

Curtis awakens to yes, another sparkling morning in Seattle, Washington. Take a look at his chest. Isn't that attractive? The phone rings; it's a WynTech administrative assistant with the news of Tom Ravell's unfortunate demise. Then somebody pounds on the front door. Say hey to Detective Powell, Curtis. Next time, man … put on a shirt first.

Curtis Craig's Apartment

Living Room

♦ Talk to Detective Powell. Looks like Curtis needs some ceiling work.

♦ Talk to Detective Powell three more times.

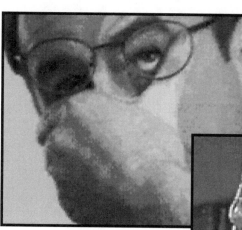

Figure 4-1. CLAW. LOOK! Those darn upstairs neighbors are at it again.

Chapter Four

Detective Powell is starting to get suspicious of Curtis, who doesn't help matters by having near-slobbering fits every time she interrogates him. Then again, I'd probably gibber a bit at the sight of The Claw, too. Curtis ends up back in his bedroom—with a shirt on, thank goodness.

Bedroom

- Look in the mirror. Curtis expresses a high opinion of himself.

- Go into the front hall.

Front Hall

- Click on the drop box to get the mail.

- Go into the living room.

Living Room

- Click today's mail on Curtis to sort it.

An Annotated Walkthrough

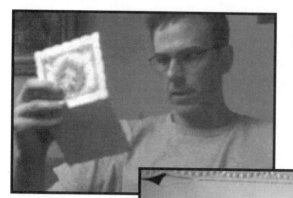

Figure 4-2. **MAIL CALL.** Full circle, eh? I hope it's not one of those places where they make you do the Hokey Pokey.

"Meet me at Borderline tonight. This time we'll go full circle. Do you dare, Curtis?
— Therese."

Curtis gets an invitation to meet Therese at the Borderline tonight. What does she mean by "full circle"? Do you dare, Curtis? He also gets a scary letter from Mom that turns into a mashed eyeball in his hand. Cool!

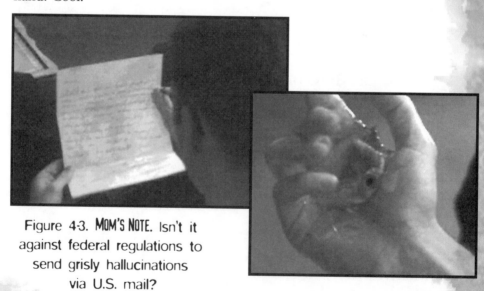

Figure 4-3. **MOM'S NOTE.** Isn't it against federal regulations to send grisly hallucinations via U.S. mail?

Chapter Four

♦ Click on the rat cage. Curtis talks to Blob.

♦ Click on the cage again.

Figure 4-4. HEARTY APPETITE. Blob's got an awfully good heart, and she's willing to share it with the world.

♦ Click on the cage one more time. Curtis's devotion to Miss Blob is touching, isn't it?

♦ Click on the bookshelf. Hey, where can I get a copy of *Pulping Heads Made Easy?*

Figure 4-5. BOOK BOXING. When in doubt, punch out your bookshelf, I always say.

♦ Use Dr. Harburg's card on the phone to make an appointment.

♦ Travel to WynTech.

Phantasmagoria: A Puzzle of Flesh

WynTech Industries

Main Hallway

♦ Enter the main office area.

Main Office Area

♦ Go to Tom Ravell's cubicle.

Detective Powell stops Curtis before he can enter. She doesn't care much for him, does she? After another appearance by the Hecatomb (in the form of post-murder Tom) and a few more stinging rebukes from the detective, Curtis ends up in the main hallway.

Figure 4-6. OLD HAMMERHEAD TOM. Curtis, I think your boss is really looking forward to your next performance review.

♦ Travel to the Dreaming Tree.

DREAMING TREE

♦ Talk to Trevor three times.

Figure 4-7.
SPLIT PERSONALITIES.
Trevor and Curtis conspire to investigate WynTech's basement secrets. Let's just hope our guys don't end up like that banana.

Trev's "Spidey-sense" tells him another murder is inevitable, and he urges Curtis to leave town for a while to ease Detective Powell's suspicions. When Curtis refuses, Trevor offers to help find out more about the Threshold project. Then conversation turns to Trevor's love life.

♦ Talk to Trevor once more. He foists his treat on Curtis.

Phantasmagoria: A Puzzle of Flesh

Ack! Did you see what I saw? Pepper on a banana split! With tastes like that, Curtis deserves everything that comes his way, as far as I'm concerned.

♦ Travel to Dr. Harburg's office.

Dr. Harburg's Office

Curtis enters the office looking a little dour. When the doctor asks what's bothering him, he replies: "Everything."

Figure 4-8. **HELP!** Curtis fears for his sanity ... and he hasn't even gotten Dr. Harburg's bill yet.

♦ After Curtis enters, click on Dr. Harburg to talk to her.

♦ Click twice on the snow-globe on her desk.

Curtis complains that something is "messing with my head." When the good doctor probes for more information, Curtis stonewalls, claiming he can't talk until he figures out what's happening.

♦ Click twice more on Dr. Harburg.

Curtis explodes with anger, storms out of the office, and Dr. Harburg's concern grows. Shaken, she documents a "psychotic episode marked by severe paranoia and irrational anger."

Figure 4-9. **END OF SESSION.** Doc Harburg wants to help, but Curtis blows up at the thought of another mental hospital, private or otherwise.

♦ Travel to Curtis's apartment.

CURTIS CRAIG'S APARTMENT

As soon as you enter, a "knocking timer" begins. After a few seconds, Jocilyn knocks on the door.

Front Hall

♦ Click on the door to answer it.

Figure 4-10. Angel of Mercy. Does Curtis deserve such loving forgiveness? *I don't think so!*

Living Room

♦ Click on Jocilyn to talk to her.

♦ Click on Jocilyn again.

Figure 4-11. GOOD OFFER. Jocilyn is badly shaken by Tom's death and wants Curtis to run away with her.

Things get tender—until Joss sees Therese's claw marks on Curtis's chest. After she storms out, Curtis ends up in the bedroom.

Bedroom

♦ Look in the mirror. Whoa!

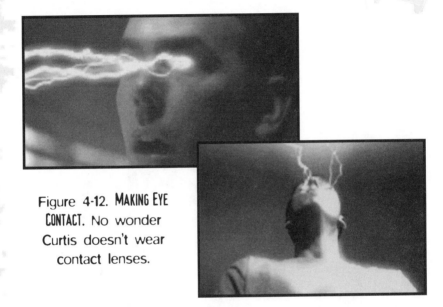

Figure 4-12. **MAKING EYE CONTACT.** No wonder Curtis doesn't wear contact lenses.

♦ Go to the living room.

Living Room

♦ Click on Jocilyn's hairpin on the coffee table for a closer view.

♦ Take the hairpin.

Figure 4-13. **JOCILYN'S HAIRPIN.** Don't miss this handy little item on your way out the door.

♦ Travel to WynTech.

WYNTECH INDUSTRIES

Main Hallway

♦ Use the hairpin on Paul Allen Warner's door. Curtis picks the lock and enters Warner's office.

Figure 4-14. LOCK PICK. Use Jocilyn's hairpin to pick the lock on Paul Allen Warner's office door.

Paul Allen Warner's Office

♦ Click on the desk for a closer view.

♦ Click on the computer.

♦ Under System Login Accounts, select "CurtisC."

♦ Type in his password: "BLOB."

♦ Click the LOG IN button.

♦ Click on the e-mail mailbox icon.

♦ Open the mail from Trevor titled "READ THIS!"

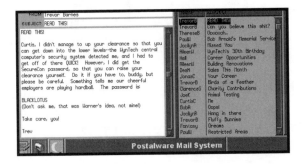

Figure 4-15. **HACK WORK.** Trevor cracks the security system password. Now Curtis can raise his security clearance level.

Trevor couldn't raise Curtis's security clearance level, but he did hack his way to the SecureCon password: "BLACKLOTUS." Now Curtis must access the security system himself to raise his security clearance level. Note Trevor's admission that WynTech's central computer's security system detected him. Uh-oh.

Phantasmagoria: A Puzzle of Flesh

- Click on the LOG OUT icon (crescent moon) and exit the system.

- Click on the computer again.

- Under System Login Accounts, select "PWarner."

- Type in Warner's password: "CARPE DIEM."

- Click the LOG IN button.

Note the new system icon—the twin computers—at the bottom of the screen. This is the SecureCon icon.

Figure 4-16. **CLEARANCE.** That twin-computer icon at the bottom of the screen gives you access to the SecureCon system—if you got the password from Trevor's e-mail.

- Click on the SecureCon icon.

- Under System Login Accounts, select "CurtisC." Note his low security level of 1.

- Click on the up-arrow next to Security Level.

- Enter the password you got from Trevor: "BLACKLOTUS."

Chapter Four

This raises Curtis's security level to 2, giving him access to WynTech's lower levels. It also triggers a nasty appearance on the monitor by the Hecatomb.

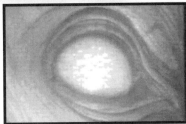

Figure 4-17. GOTCHA! But who's got who? Curtis raises his security level ... but something's got its eye on him.

♦ Exit the computer interface.

♦ Try to open the desk drawer. Locked!

♦ Use the screwdriver to open the desk drawer.

♦ Take the piece of paper on the left side of the drawer.

It's a speech to be given by Paul Allen Warner. Note the highlighted passages—"10/9/58" and "Threshold basement."

Good evening, ladies and gentlemen.

We at WynTech are so pleased you could be here tonight. As you all probably know, the Threshold project was begun October 9, 1958 (10/9/58), with the discovery of the natural anomaly known as the Threshold in the basement of the old Donner building. Back then, we were dealing with something we knew nothing about; a strange, inexplicable force which seemed useless and untamable. But there were men with vision then, as there are now, who saw the potential of that little miracle in the basement.

Figure 4-18. WARNER'S DRAWER. Curtis finds a piece of paper and a codebook in Warner's office desk drawer. Note the "highlights" of the speech—a code to access an important area.

♦ Take the codebook on the right side of the drawer.

♦ Exit the drawer close-up.

♦ In inventory, examine the codebook. Its title: *A Child's Introduction to Secret Codes.*

♦ In close-up view, open the book.

Note the highlighted chapter title in the book's Table of Contents: "The Rosetta Stone." As I'm sure you guessed, this bit of information will be important later.

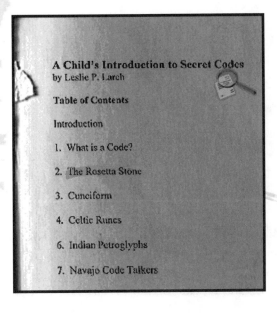

A Child's Introduction to Secret Codes
by Leslie P. Larch

Table of Contents

Introduction

1. What is a Code?

2. The Rosetta Stone

3. Cuneiform

4. Celtic Runes

6. Indian Petroglyphs

7. Navajo Code Talkers

Figure 4-19. CODEBOOK. Looks like Warner never got past the Table of Contents.

♦ Exit the desktop close-up to the left.

♦ Click on the door to exit into the main hallway.

Main Hallway

♦ Go down the hallway to the glass door.

♦ Use Curtis's card key on the key sensor at right. The glass doors open and Curtis proceeds to the elevator.

Figure 4-20. **THROUGH A GLASS DARKLY.** After Curtis hacks into the security system and raises his security clearance, his card key gives him access to the lower levels of WynTech.

♦ Use Curtis's card key on the key sensor just left of the elevator doors. Curtis rides down to the lower level corridors of Wyntech.

Lower Level Corridors

♦ Click on the double doors ahead of Curtis. Curtis goes through and has a quick flashback.

Figure 4-21. **FLASHBACK #1.** Warner and Jonas Craig watch something bright and important.

Chapter Four

♦ Click on the garment on the floor in front of Curtis. It's a strait-jacket—and it triggers another flashback.

Curtis sees a babbling mental patient dragged past Paul Allen Warner toward a pulsing light source. But the patient suffers a heart attack. An angry Warner says, "We're running out of time! It's going to close!" Then he orders Jonas Craig, Curtis's father, to ask Dr. Marek for "another one—quickly."

Figure 4-22.
FLASHBACK #2. Oops,
lost another one.
Man, they just don't
make human
guinea pigs like
they used to.

♦ Click on the next doorway. Curtis goes through to the next hall.

♦ Click on the toy on the floor.

Curtis has yet another flashback—his father, hurrying out of the Threshold room past Curtis as a young boy. This continues the previous scene. Jonas is hurrying off to get another test subject. The boy Curtis watches him go—"Daddy?"—and then wanders into the Threshold room.

An Annotated Walkthrough

Figure 4-23. CURIOUS CURTIS. You know, Jonas, it's probably not a good idea to let your son play near interdimensional rips in the fabric of the space-time continuum.

♦ Go through the next doorway. Another flashback!

♦ Click on the blanket on the floor.

This time, Curtis flashes back to his distraught father, cradling a blanketed young Curtis in his arms. Note Curtis's hand. It's covered with some sort of slime.

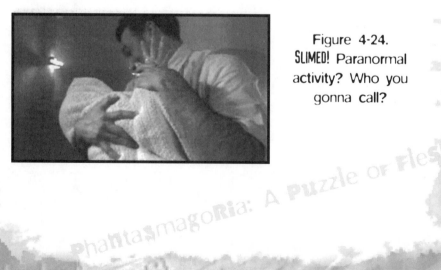

Figure 4-24. SLIMED! Paranormal activity? Who you gonna call?

Chapter Four

♦ Approach the door at the end of the corridor.

♦ Click on the door. It's locked.

♦ Click on the keypad to the right of the door for a closer view.

♦ Enter the code.

What code? Check out the speech you filched from Warner's desk drawer. Remember the highlighted segments? Two words, "Threshold" and "basement." And a date: "October 9, 1958." That date is the entry code.

♦ Enter "10958" in the keypad. Curtis enters the underground computer room.

Figure 4-25. THRESHOLD ROOM ENTRY CODE

Underground Computer Room

♦ Click on the computer. Curtis sits down and turns it on. The Secure System requests a password.

♦ Type in the password from the codebook: "ROSETTA."

An Annotated Walkthrough

Figure 4-26. CURTIS AT THE HELM. Looks like the bridge on a starship. Enter the password—"ROSETTA"—to fire up this rig.

A message! But from who? The correspondent greets "PAWarner" and offers regrets about the inability to synthesize a chemical compound. He/she requests a list of needed ingredients—including "two live adult human creatures." Sounds like something an inhuman alien might say. The correspondent also asks about the status of something called "the Twin."

♦ Select responses to the alien communications by pushing the buttons at right.

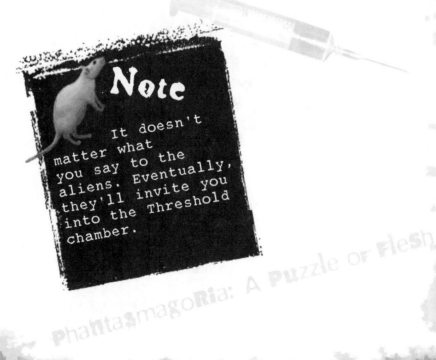

Note

It doesn't matter what you say to the aliens. Eventually, they'll invite you into the Threshold chamber.

Figure 4-27. **INTERDIMENSIONAL CHAT ROOM.** Doesn't matter what you say to these alien guys. Sooner or later they invite you in for a face-to-face (or face-to-whatever) chat.

♦ Keep pushing buttons until the aliens respond, "We do not understand your meaning. Please enter Threshold transport and commence communication."

♦ Press the EXIT button.

♦ Click on the access panel at right. Looks like another key sensor.

Caution

Don't use Curtis's card key on the key sensor at the bottom of the access panel! If you do, you end up in the cemetery. Curtis can never use his card, regardless of his security level. He'll need to be someone else.

- Exit the underground computer room.

Lower Level Corridors

- Follow the corridors back to the elevator.

- Click on the elevator call panel to ride the elevator back up to WynTech's main level.

Main Hallway

- Exit WynTech.

- Travel to the Borderline.

BORDERLINE CLUB

Main Dance Area

- Talk to the patron at the bar.

Figure 4-28.
TOP SPIN.
"Therese is going to eat you alive, Pop Tart."

♦ Try to go into the rest room.

♦ Join Therese in the booth.

Booth

♦ Talk to Therese.

♦ Talk to Therese again. Like a good writer, her motto is: "Show, don't tell."

♦ Click on the drink in front of Curtis. He sucks it up and follows Therese from the booth.

Main Dance Area

- Veer right to follow Therese.

- Click on the back door. The bouncer stops Curtis again.

- Take the Borderline invitation from inventory.

- Use the invitation on the bouncer. This time, he lets Curtis proceed.

- Click on the puzzle below the door window for a closer view.

Figure 4-29. BY INVITATION ONLY. Take another peek at Therese's note for a clue to the Pit's door puzzle.

Tip

Puzzle Solution Hint: Remember Therese's cryptic comment on the Borderline invitation? She wrote: "This time we'll go full circle."

To solve the puzzle:

Click on the four square puzzle pieces until the green quarter-circles face toward the middle of the puzzle. Then click on the middle of the puzzle. The pieces slide together, forming a green circle—as in, "we'll go full circle"—in the middle of the puzzle.

Figure 4-30. "THE PIT" DOOR PUZZLE SOLUTION

Phantasmagoria: A Puzzle of Flesh

"The Pit" (Back Room)

♦ Click on the rack of stuff hanging at the far right. Curtis pulls a rope to reveal a bondage hood.

♦ Click on the curtains to pull them aside.

Boo! Oh, it's just Therese. OK, parents, time to dim that monitor if you're playing the "More Intense" version in the family room.

Figure 4-31. RESTRAINED PERFORMANCE. Well, the audience liked it, anyway. Back at home, Curtis finds a little memento of his doomed relationship with Therese.

Chapter Four

After the "performance," the scene shifts to Curtis's apartment, where he staggers into bed once again … and discovers the bondage hood stashed in his sheets. Ah, memories. Cut back to the Borderline bathroom, where Therese has some *real* bondage activity with the Hecatomb. And thus ends Chapter 4.

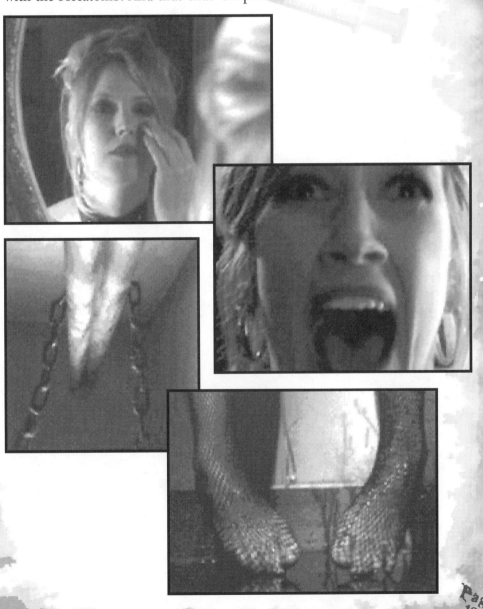

An Annotated Walkthrough

Chapter

Chapter
Chapter
Chapter

Chapter 5

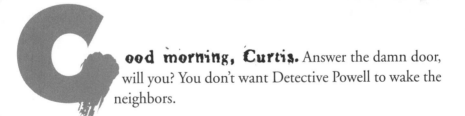

Good morning, Curtis. Answer the damn door, will you? You don't want Detective Powell to wake the neighbors.

Phantasmagoria: A Puzzle of Flesh

CURTIS CRAIG'S APARTMENT

Living Room

◆ Click on Detective Powell to talk to her.

◆ Click on the rat cage. Curtis notices that Blob is missing … and then finds her.

◆ Talk to Detective Powell twice more.

Gosh, looks like Curtis has a friend for life! The scene automatically shifts to the bedroom, where Curtis is dressed and ready for action.

Bedroom

A quick check of your inventory reveals that certain items are missing—wallet, WynTech card key, and Dr. Harburg's business card. Where'd they go? We'll find out shortly.

◆ Look in the dresser mirror.

◆ Look in the mirror again. Therese?

Chapter Five

Figure 5-1. **AX MAN.** Who is that guy? He looks vaguely familiar.

♦ Go into the front hall.

Front Hall

♦ Check the drop box for mail. Nothing at first, but then …

♦ Turn and get the mail. Curtis gets an odd morphing note and ends up in the living room.

Figure 5-2. **SOON!** Curtis gets a mysterious, morphing note in his drop box. Looks like somebody knows this is the last chapter of the game.

♦ Go into the bedroom.

Phantasmagoria: A Puzzle of Flesh

Note

You can't leave the apartment until Curtis finds his wallet.

Bedroom

♦ Go right to the nightstand.

♦ Open the nightstand drawer for a closer view.

Figure 5-3. **MISSING WALLET.** Curtis left his wallet in the nightstand drawer this morning.

♦ Take the wallet.

♦ Exit the close-up.

♦ Go back into the living room.

Living Room

♦ Click on Blob's cage.

♦ Use Dr. Harburg's card on the phone to call for an emergency appointment.

Figure 5-4.
REALITY CHECK. Make it out to Dr. Rikki Harburg.

Note

You won't have Dr. Harburg's card until you get Curtis's wallet from the nightstand drawer.

This triggers a long sequence in which Dr. Harburg makes the appointment with Curtis (who sounds like a paranoid raving lunatic—"They're *all* in on it, Doc!"); arranges for a security presence; finds that her phone is bugged, and receives a visit from your friendly neighborhood Hecatomb.

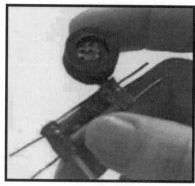

Figure 5-5. PHONE FIND. Dr. Harburg is really bugged. But that's the least of her problems, as it turns out.

DR. HARBURG'S OFFICE

Curtis arrives to find the office in disarray. What's that stuff smeared over the wall behind the desk?

Figure 5-6. OFFICE CALL. Slime on the wall, phone off the hook. Doesn't look good, does it?

Chapter Five

- Click on the phone hanging off the edge of the desk. Curtis picks it up and hears Dr. Harburg screaming.

- Move the cursor over the desk until it becomes a down arrow, and then click.

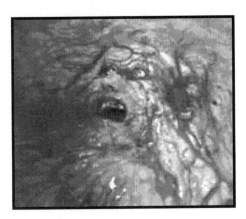

Figure 5-7. DOC SOUP. Throw in a few lentils and some curry and you'd have a rare delicacy. In certain dimensions, anyway.

Wow! Somebody melted down Doc Harburg. And that somebody makes an immediate appearance. Yes, it's the Hecatomb, looking like the weird, spiky, other-dimensional being he is. A security guard enters and holds Curtis at gunpoint. But then he takes a peek at the doc. *Now's your chance!*

Figure 5-8. **PRIVATE VISION.** Curtis sees the Hecatomb, but the security guard doesn't.

♦ *Quickly!* Make a break for the door. (If you wait too long, Curtis takes a bullet.)

♦ Travel to WynTech.

WynTech Industries

♦ Enter the main office area.

Main Office Area

♦ Get a drink from the water cooler. *Mmmm,* mutant squid juice.

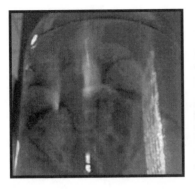

Figure 5-9. MORE FUN AT THE WATER COOLER.

♦ Go to Curtis's cubicle.

Curtis Craig's Cubicle

♦ Sit in the chair.

♦ Click on the computer for a nice conversation with the Hecatomb.

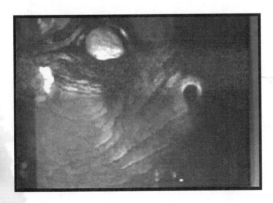

Figure 5-10. INTERACTIVE TV. Don't get so whacked out, Curtis. He just wants what's best for you.

♦ Exit Curtis's cubicle and go to Bob's cubicle.

Bob Arnold's Cubicle

♦ Click on the magnifying glass sitting on the keyboard.

Figure 5-11. BOB AGONISTES. Hi, Bob! You know, I can't understand a word you're saying when you shriek like that.

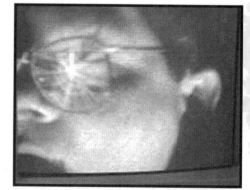

♦ Go to Tom Ravell's cubicle.

Tom Ravell's Cubicle

♦ Click on Tom's computer.

♦ Go to Paul Allen Warner's office.

Chapter Five

Paul Allen Warner's Office

♦ Click on the desktop for a closer view.

♦ Click on the computer.

♦ Log on as "CurtisC." Remember, his password is "BLOB."

♦ Read all the new e-mail for Curtis.

In particular, read the mail from Trevor titled "Forget Wyntech." The correspondence from Marianne Craig, Curtis's long-dead mother, is kind of interesting, too. Note her repetition of "*Soon! Soon! Soon!*" It echoes the mysterious, morphing letter left in Curtis's mail drop back at the apartment earlier. Apparently, something big is about to happen.

♦ Log out, then log on again as "PWarner," using his password: "CARPE DIEM."

♦ Open the "PaulW" folder.

♦ Open the "goldmine.doc" file and read it.

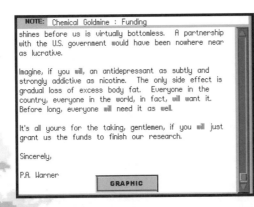

> **NOTE:** Chemical Goldmine : Funding
>
> shines before us is virtually bottomless. A partnership with the U.S. government would have been nowhere near as lucrative.
>
> Imagine, if you will, an antidepressant as subtly and strongly addictive as nicotine. The only side effect is gradual loss of excess body fat. Everyone in the country, everyone in the world, in fact, will want it. Before long, everyone will need it as well.
>
> It's all yours for the taking, gentlemen, if you will just grant us the funds to finish our research.
>
> Sincerely,
>
> P.A. Warner
>
> GRAPHIC

Figure 5-12. DRUG STORE. Dimensional rip? Threshold dwellers? What's going on here?

Suddenly, much is clear. Warner wants to push the ultimate addiction—a drug that makes you happy and skinny. Indeed, WynTech's greed is exceeded only by its hubris in assuming it can control both the dimensional rip and the activities of these so-called "Threshold dwellers."

♦ Click on the Graphic button. The Threshold drug logo appears.

♦ Click on the Print button. A computer printout of the Threshold document appears in your inventory.

Figure 5-13. THRESHOLD LOGO.
This computer printout will
be helpful later.

♦ Exit into the main hallway.

Main Hallway

♦ Go into the Network Room—and brace yourself.

Network Room

Trevor surprises Curtis. He explains he's been delving deep into the company network—deeper than you've just delved, apparently. Trev knows that WynTech is synthesizing illegal drugs; but he also claims "they've killed before." He tells Curtis he's going to the police. And then all hell breaks loose.

Note

Important: When Trevor holds up his card key, note that he says, "I gave myself top clearance."

Figure 5-14. WIRED. Trevor gave himself top security clearance. Apparently, this makes Network Room cables very angry.

After the long and horrific scene, click on Trevor. Curtis checks to see if he's still alive; and we finally meet the Hecatomb, face-to-slimy-face.

Figure 5-15. BLOODY MARIONETTE. The Hecatomb sure gets a kick out of slaughter.

♦ Click on Trevor again to get his security card key.

Figure 5-16. HIGH CARD. There's Trevor's WynTech card key. Don't leave home without it.

After you take Trevor's card key, Curtis ends up in the main hallway.

Main Hallway

♦ Go to the glass doors.

♦ Use Curtis's card key on the key sensor.

♦ At the elevator, use Curtis's card key on the key sensor to ride down to WynTech's lower level.

Chapter Five

Lower Level Corridors

◆ Go through the first doors.

Curtis touches slime on the inner door handle—and flashes back to his boyhood emergence from the Threshold.

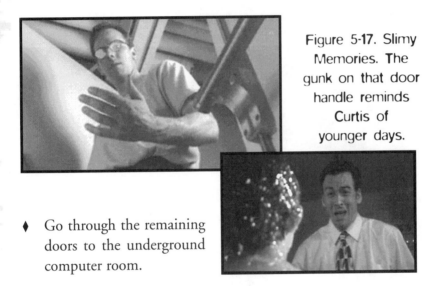

Figure 5-17. Slimy Memories. The gunk on that door handle reminds Curtis of younger days.

◆ Go through the remaining doors to the underground computer room.

Underground Computer Room

◆ Click on the computer. Curtis sits at the console.

◆ Enter the password: "Rosetta."

◆ Click on buttons to converse with the aliens until they suggest you "enter the Threshold transport and commence communication."

Note

My favorite response path is to click repeatedly on the No button. This prompts the aliens to respond, we do not understand your refusal. We suspect you are "angry". I love these guys!

♦ Click the Exit button.

♦ Click on the access panel across the room for a closer view.

♦ Use Trevor's card key—*not Curtis's*—on the key sensor at the bottom of the panel.

The panel opens to reveal four icons with buttons. Do any of the icons look familiar? Yes, of course. The second from the left is the logo from the Threshold computer printout in your inventory.

Figure 5-18.
FAMILIAR ICON.
Push the button
below the
Threshold logo to
open the door.

♦ Click on the button beneath Threshold icon (second from left).

Threshold Room (WynTech)

♦ Click on the console near Curtis.

After you hear the alien voice, Paul Allen Warner appears behind Curtis and holds him at gunpoint.

Figure 5-19. **WAGES OF FEAR.**
Once again, upper
management shows
its true colors.

♦ Click on Warner.

Warner admits killing Curtis's father, Jonas, explaining that "not everyone is strong enough to accept the sacrifice of human subjects for research." Then he makes a cryptic comment about Jonas not getting his little boy back.

♦ Click on Warner again.

Figure 5-20. **ROOTS REVEALED.** Does Curtis really want to hear the truth from Warner?

Warner gleefully explains that he tossed the *real* Curtis Craig into the Threshold, and claims the human boy never returned. Instead, a "twin" emerged, an alien-engineered entity that grew to become the Curtis the Technical Writer, "some kind of imitation human … put together out of slime, dead rats, and a little bit of Curtis's brain tissue." (Which pretty much describes all tech writers.) Apparently, the human Curtis is trapped in Dimension X.

And then—guess who appears?

♦ Click on the Hecatomb. He introduces himself as—Curtis Craig!

Here's where we get the whole bitter story behind the Hecatomb's merciless haunting of Curtis. He's jealous! When Curtis hears the truth, he's sympathetic. But that only makes the Hecatomb more angry.

Chapter Five

Figure 5-21. THRILLER. OK, he's a Hecatomb.

♦ Click on the Hecatomb again.

Monster boy zaps Curtis with green lightning from the eyes of ...
his mother's decapitated head!

Figure 5-22. MOMMABOLTS.
The Hecatomb's a
pretty bitter guy. Of
course, you'd be
cranky too if you lived
on cannibalized body
parts and no sleep for
20 years. But isn't it a
little harsh to zap a
guy with his own
mom's head?

♦ Click on the Threshold control panel (center of screen).

Curtis manages to activate the Threshold and escape by leaping into the alien dimension.

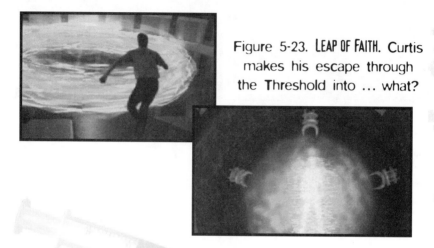

Figure 5-23. **LEAP OF FAITH.** Curtis makes his escape through the Threshold into … what?

ALIEN DIMENSION

Threshold Room (Alien)

Welcome to the land of the flying sucker fish. Seriously, *keep moving* in this dimension. Otherwise, you end up as an energy snack for a bunch of disgusting little slugs. (Thank God for that Try Again option each time you die.)

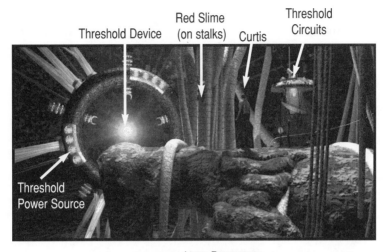

Figure 5-24. ALIEN THRESHOLD

♦ Click on the clump of big stalks right in front of Curtis for a closer view.

♦ Take some of the red slime. It appears in your inventory as "alien slime."

Figure 5-25. SLIME SOURCE. Click on those big stalks just to the left of Curtis (see figure 5-24), then grab a handful of alien slime.

An Annotated Walkthrough

- Climb down from the Threshold ledge. See that alien being just to the left of Curtis?

- Click on the weird, salami-shaped creature for a close-up.

- Take the alien creature.

- Go right twice. Another creature! (There, behind Curtis.)

- Click on the odd, bubble-like creature for a closer view.

- Take the alien creature.

- For fun, try to combine the two alien creatures (salami and bubble) in inventory.

Figure 5-26. **ODD COMBO.** They look harmless enough. If you try to "mate" them in inventory, they give it the old college try—but the chemistry's just not there.

- Go right again. More beings. God, they're cute.

- Take the starfish-shaped alien creature at right.

Chapter Five

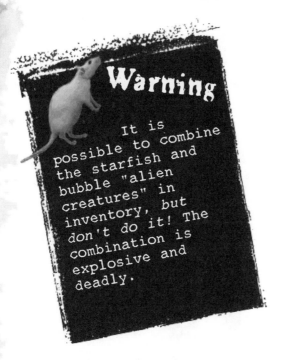

Warning

It is possible to combine the starfish and bubble "alien creatures" in inventory, but don't do it! The combination is explosive and deadly.

♦ Click on the creatures at left for a closer view.

Bubbly neon things chew on pink stuff before they scurry away. Hey, wouldn't it be cool to catch an electric alien? Apparently, they feed on that pink alien fungus. Better grab a handful of the stuff.

♦ In the close-up, take some alien fungus.

Figure 5-27.
FUNGUS AMONG US. Grab a starfish, then scoop up a handful of pink fungus. Note that electric bubble beings fed on the fungus.

♦ In inventory, examine the starfish-shaped creature more closely. Leave the close-up window open.

♦ Take the salami-shaped creature from inventory and click it on the close-up of the starfish-shaped creature.

Wow! The two creatures combine in some sort of symbiotic relationship. Your inventory cleverly labels them "combined alien creatures."

Chapter Five

Figure 5-28. Symbiosis.
What do you get when
you combine a salami
with a starfish?
Answer: A turnip!

♦ Turn right.

♦ Veer left through that
cave opening.

Energy Plume Room

Curtis discovers an incredible plume of energy rising up a giant shaft; it looks like a reverse waterfall. An electrical barrier surrounds the green plume.

♦ Click low on the plume. Watch alien creatures fly into the electrical barrier and eviscerate. (This is a hint.)

Figure 5-29. DUST TO DUST. A deadly electric wall blocks access to that rising energy plume. Touch it and you're cinders, man.

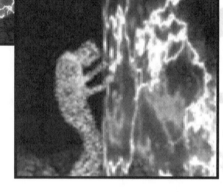

Warning

Don't click more than once on the electrical barrier! If you do, Curtis gets toasted into antidimensional ash.

♦ Click *high up* on the plume.

See how those alien creatures fly over the top of the electrical barrier? Note also how they fly directly into the energy plume—and seem to rise harmlessly up the shaft! If that doesn't look like fun, I don't know what does.

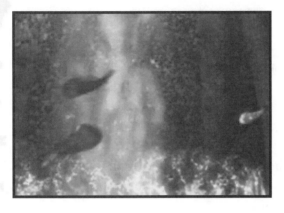

Figure 5-30. GOING UP? Alien flying fish fly into the plume and ride it up the shaft.

♦ Turn left. A couple more electric bubble-beings lurk near the cave opening.

♦ Click on them for a closer view. They scurry away—all except one.

Aren't those the same guys who were munching on pink fungus earlier? The answer, of course, is yes.

♦ Take the alien fungus from inventory and click it on the remaining electric alien. Curtis places some fungus as bait.

♦ In the ensuing close-up shot, click on the electric alien to take it.

Figure 5-31. SHOCKING CREATURE. This hungry little being fairly glows with energy.

- Turn back to the energy plume.

- Take the "combined alien creatures" from inventory and click them on the electrical barrier.

The ravenous little tuber chews a hole in the barrier. The hole stays open just long enough for Curtis to hop through, and then closes behind our boy. Now what?

- Click on the plume at the far right side of the screen. Curtis takes the express elevator to the upper level.

Hecatomb Room

See that fellow encased in alien crud across the room? That, apparently, is the real Curtis Craig. He's totally *wired*, man.

- Approach the encased body.

- Click on the encased body to trigger the endgame sequence.

Figure 5-32. CURTIS, MEET CURTIS. OK, maybe *our* Curtis is just a blob of protoplasm, but the real Curtis doesn't look much better.

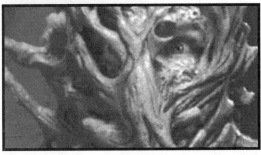

The Hecatomb suddenly appears and zaps Curtis into a bizarre series of interactive flashbacks. They unfold in quick succession, so prepare to move fast.

MENTAL HOSPITAL: OPERATING ROOM

Dr. Marek preps Curtis for vivisection. He wants to see "what little mutant boys are made of."

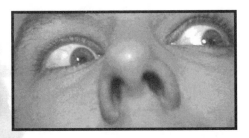

Figure 5-33. WHERE AM I? Curtis awakens to find himself on Dr. Marek's operating table.

◆ Click on the surgical tray for a closer view.

◆ Click on the big syringe. Curtis spikes the good doctor. And we're off to the Dreaming Tree.

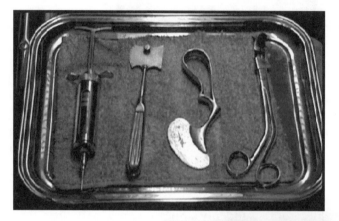

Figure 5-34. **TEMPLE SHOT**. Grab that big syringe and give the doc a big, big headache.

DREAMING TREE

Jocilyn loves Curtis *sooooo* much. Enough to kill the bastard for his humiliating indiscretions.

Figure 5-35. GUNPOINT REDUX. And thus Curtis stares down a gun barrel for the third time in Chapter 5.

♦ Click *directly* on the gun to end the threat. WynTech is next.

WYNTECH INDUSTRIES: MAIN HALLWAY

What happened to WynTech? Things are dangling—tubing, wires, pipes, coworkers' appendages. Yes, those are zombies—Trevor, Tom, and Bob. And they're pretty angry at Curtis. As Curtis scrambles backward, he slips on some of Bob's discarded viscera—what a slob!—and drops his card key.

Note

Move quickly! This sequence is on a timer.

♦ Quickly! When the action stops, look down; that is, move the cursor until it becomes a down arrow, and then click. You see a close-up view of the card key.

♦ Quickly! Grab the card key.

Figure 5-36.
LET'S DO LUNCH!
But first, let me grab my card key. I'll meet you upstairs, OK?

♦ Quickly! Click on the elevator door at right (just above Bob's head) for a close-up of the key sensor.

♦ Quickly! Use Curtis' card key on the key sensor.

Fortunately, zombies stagger at a slow pace, or Curtis would be dead meat…or maybe live meat, I don't know. In any case, your next destination is the bondage rack in the Pit room of the Borderline.

BORDERLINE CLUB

Yee-ha! Therese, inhabited by none other than the Hecatomb, straddles Curtis and *rides that dogie!* She's having entirely too much fun, so she decides to zap Curtis with other-dimensional death bolts. Gosh, how will our hero escape this one?

♦ Click on the handle of the bondage rack. It's at the far left.

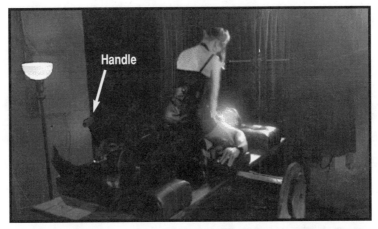

Figure 5-37. RACK 'EM! If you don't pull that rack handle soon, Therese will make mincemeat of poor Curtis.

Curtis dumps Heca-Therese, giving her a taste of her own medicine. Sounds kind of unpleasant. Curtis ends up in his boyhood backyard.

LITTLE CURTIS'S BACKYARD

Hi Mom! Could you do something about those hedges? They could use a trim.

♦ Click on Curtis' mom to hug her. Family values rule!

ALIEN DIMENSION

Hecatomb Room

When Curtis returns from his hugfest with mom, he finds the Hecatomb losing power. And the real Curtis is getting just a *little* nervous over there.

♦ Click on the encased body.

Figure 5-39. **NO REMORSE.** Curtis wastes no time in eliminating his evil tormentor.

Curtis rips out his evil twin's life support. The room crumbles a bit, and a doorway opens. Guess what? It leads back down to the Threshold room. But don't leave yet.

♦ Click on the encased body again.

♦ Click on the gold slime on the torso. Your inventory calls it "alien glop."

♦ Turn left.

♦ Click on the cave opening to exit the room.

Chapter Five

Threshold Room (Alien)

♦ Go left.

♦ Click on the big pipe just to the right of Curtis for a closer view.

Uh-oh. That pipe looks damaged. No dimensional rip could operate with that kind of power leakage. We'd better do some patch work.

Figure 5-40. **POWER LEAK.** That torn pipe near Curtis is draining power from the Threshold device. Mix up some alien ooze to patch it.

♦ In inventory, examine the "alien slime." Leave the close-up window open.

♦ Take the "alien glop" and click it on the alien slime in the close-up window to create "alien ooze."

♦ Click on the torn pipe for a closer view.

♦ Use the "alien ooze" to seal the ripped pipe.

♦ Climb up the ledge to the Threshold device.

♦ Click on the green power source globes at the far left. (See figure 5-24.)

In the close-up, you can see that one of the Threshold power source globes is out of commission. If Curtis wants to escape back to a dimension where good Sierra games are available, he must find a way to replace the power source so he can power up the Alien Threshold.

Figure 5-41. POWER OUT. You need a new power globe for the Threshold device. Check your inventory for an unusual source of electricity.

Chapter Five

♦ Take the "electric alien" from inventory and click it on the unlit globe. *Voila!*

♦ Step back from the power source globes.

♦ Click on the Threshold circuitry hanging just behind Curtis. (See figure 5-42.)

♦ Click on the viewscreen in the middle of the console for a closer view.

Figure 5-42.
THRESHOLD CONSOLE.
Click on this viewscreen to see the Alien Threshold circuitry.

How to Reconnect the Threshold Circuits

Here's the weirdest Rube Goldberg circuit wiring job you'll ever do. See the two batches of unattached wires coming out of that blue "sausage" at the far right? You must reattach those wires to the circuit nodes, and then fire up all components of the mechanism.

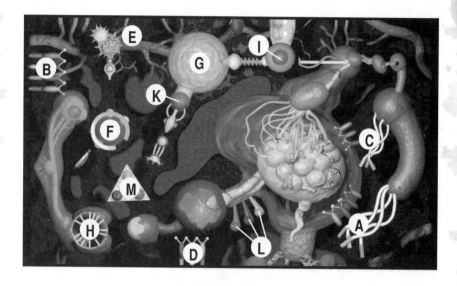

Figure 5-43. THRESHOLD CIRCUITRY

In the following steps, the letters A to M refer to the call-outs on figure 5-43:

1. Plug the four wires at the lower right (A on figure 5-43) into the correct circuit nodes. To do this, simply click on each wire, drag it to the correct node, and click again to plug it in.

Don't match the wire colors to the circuit plug colors! Instead, duplicate the correctly wired circuits at the upper left of the circuit board (B). I list the correct connections in the following table.

Table Four-Wire Circuit

Wire Color	Node Color
Purple	Green
Orange	Blue
Green	Purple
Blue	Red

2. Plug in the three wires at the far right of the circuit board (C). Again, simply click on each wire, drag it to the correct circuit node, and click again.

   As in step 1, do not match wire color to circuit node color. Instead, duplicate the correctly wired circuits at the bottom of the circuit board (D). I list the correct connections in the following table.

Table Three-Wire Circuit

Wire Color	Node Color
Orange	Purple
Green	Red
Purple	Green

3. Click on the laser knob (E). This fires a laser into a laser deflector ball (F) and starts the power flow into the Threshold mechanism. Now you must redirect the power flow to activate all components of the mechanism.

4. Click once on the laser deflector ball (F). It rotates counterclockwise.

5. Click on the laser knob (E). This activates the green power orb (G).

Phantasmagoria: A Puzzle of Flesh

6. Click on the laser deflector ball (F). It rotates counterclockwise again.

7. Click on the laser knob (E). This activates the wheel (H) at the lower left of the circuit board.

8. Click on the power redirection knob (I). The knob's red arrow now points right, indicating the power flow's direction; this also activates the egg-shaped conduit (J).

9. Click again on the power redirection knob (I). The knob's red arrow now points left, redirecting power through the green power orb. This activates the power button (K).

10. Click on the laser knob (E) again and notice the three switches (L). They flash in the following order—red, yellow, blue.

11. Click on the three switches (L) in that order—again, red, yellow, blue. Nothing seems to happen, but you've made another connection.

12. Click twice on the triangle (M) embedded with the three gems. This rotates the blue gem to the lower right corner of the triangle.

13. Click on the power button (K) to zap a power bolt through the triangle's blue gem and off a mirror into the wheel (H). This in turn sends a power surge across the gap—and your circuit connection is complete.

Curtis steps through the Threshold and returns to our dimension.

Figure 5-45. ZAPPED BACK. Once you repair the Threshold circuits and fire up the device, Curtis automatically takes leave of Dimension X.

WynTech Industries

Threshold Room

Jocilyn waits for Curtis on the other side. Our hero now faces a difficult choice. He can continue his life as a human with a gorgeous loving girlfriend, despite knowing that he is indeed an other-dimensional alien, or he can return to the dimension of his origin and live out his life with a bunch of ugly slime guys and mutant sucker fish. Go ahead, decide. Take your time. I'll give you five seconds.

Figure 5-46. MOMENT OF TRUTH. Which do you pick? Jocilyn? Or slime? Tough choice.

♦ If you want to be an alien, click on the swirling Threshold.

♦ If you want to be a human, click on Jocilyn.

Watch the game-ending movie. Congratulations! Hang around to view Paul Allen Warner's fate, which screens after the game credits run.

Phantasmagoria: A Puzzle of Flesh

Phantasmagoria: A Puzzle of Flesh

A Conversation with Lorelei Shannon

You might think the author/designer of a game like *Phantasmagoria: A Puzzle of Flesh* spends a lot of time on the twilight edge of reality. Picture Morticia Addams slinking around a candlelit apartment. Black furniture, black clothes. Odd pentagrams on the wall. And then there's that "closet"…

Unfortunately, I can't give you the definitive report on Lorelei Shannon, horror queen; our interview took place via telephone. I didn't think it was too appropriate to call a total stranger and ask, "What are you wearing right now?" But the truth is, she sounded *awfully* normal. Her infant son, two-and-a-half weeks old, cooed on her lap. Happy dogs barked in the background. Given the game we were discussing, it was a dissociative moment. I needed Dr. Rikki Harburg to sort things out.

But then I remembered: This is the same woman who wrote the aggressively cute *King's Quest VII: The Princeless Bride*. It gave me a chill. Really, that kind of range in a writer is scarier than a whole bunch of Hecatombs.

An Annotated Walkthrough

RICK BARBA: Start by telling us about your background. How did you come to be a game designer at Sierra?

LORELEI SHANNON: Well, I've always been a writer—mostly science fiction and horror stuff. I started out in the gaming industry doing "play-by-mail" games at a tiny company called Flying Buffalo in Scottsdale, Arizona. They really started play-by-mail, and it was pretty much the precursor of online gaming.

From there I went to Sierra. Actually, my husband was hired there first, and then I joined as a copy writer for the Sierra Online magazine. After about a year of doing that … (laughs) … well, I'd finish my work and spend a lot of time doing extra work for the designers. So I ended up as a designer. I'd done a lot of game design before in face-to-face gaming.

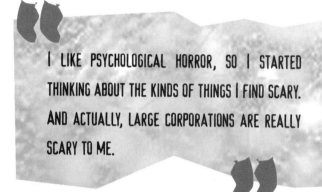

> I LIKE PSYCHOLOGICAL HORROR, SO I STARTED THINKING ABOUT THE KINDS OF THINGS I FIND SCARY. AND ACTUALLY, LARGE CORPORATIONS ARE REALLY SCARY TO ME.

RICK BARBA: Didn't you codesign *King's Quest VII* with Roberta Williams?

LORELEI SHANNON: Yes. My first game was *Pepper's Adventures in Time*, which was a collaboration with a lot of people. Then I did *King's Quest VII* with Roberta. We designed it together, and I actually wrote all of it. Then I went on to *Phantasmagoria 2*. (laughs) It's all mine.

A Conversation with Lorelei Shannon

RICK BARBA: Tell us about the genesis of your game. Where did the concept and story came from, and how did it develop?

LORELEI SHANNON: When I was offered *Phantasmagoria 2*, my first thought was, "I want to do something entirely different." The first *Phantasmagoria* is cool and everything, but it's just not my style of horror. I like psychological horror, things that are more on the edge and out there. The first *Phantasmagoria* is more of a typical haunted-house kind of story.

So I started thinking about the kinds of things I find scary. And actually, large corporations are really scary to me. (laughs) What would happen if you had haunted-house–type, scary, horrible things going on in some place like that? I love films like *Jacob's Ladder*, where weird things happen just out of the blue. So I came up with this character and started tormenting the hell out of him. Poor guy. I wanted a male protagonist, partly because it's a challenge to write from a male point of view, and partly because I get tired of seeing females chased around the house in their underwear. Hey, let's chase a guy around the house in his underwear. (laughs)

I wanted to have a play environment that was completely unsettling. I love Edgar Allan Poe's idea of the unreliable narrator, where you don't know whether this person is losing it or whether they're on the level or what. What we've created, I think, is a situation where the player is not going to know what's real and what isn't, right up until the last minute. Is Curtis guilty of a series of murders or not? I really wanted that kind of mystery element.

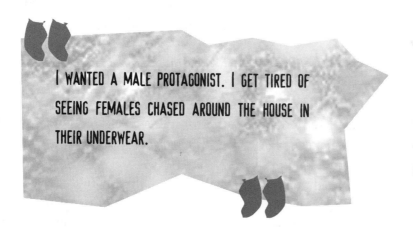

"I WANTED A MALE PROTAGONIST. I GET TIRED OF SEEING FEMALES CHASED AROUND THE HOUSE IN THEIR UNDERWEAR."

RICK BARBA: Once you came up with the game concept and the basic story line, how did the development proceed?

LORELEI SHANNON: With an interactive game this size, I like to come up with the concept, story, and characters first. I actually write out the story line, the sequence of events as they go along. Of course, as I move through the story, I'll have puzzle ideas. So I'll include the basic sketch of a puzzle here or there. But not until I've completed the story line will I go back and completely work the puzzles into the game.

That process is going to be completely different in a strategy game or a shooter, of course. But in a game like *Phantasmagoria: A Puzzle of Flesh,* where we wanted to create a realistic environment, we devised puzzles that would fit in without seeming off the wall. In a *King's Quest* you can throw in just about anything—a magic this, or an enchanted that. In this, it was more of a challenge to put in puzzles that wouldn't make the player stop and go, "Oh, yeah, right." The challenge was to weave the puzzles into the story.

RICK BARBA: Did you write a screenplay-type script for the thing?

LORELEI SHANNON: Yes. Very large, very much of a pain-in-the-neck. Lots of reference numbers.

> IN A KING'S QUEST YOU CAN THROW IN JUST ABOUT ANYTHING—A MAGIC THIS, AN ENCHANTED THAT. IN PHANTASMAGORIA, IT WAS MORE OF A CHALLENGE TO PUT IN PUZZLES THAT WOULDN'T MAKE THE PLAYER STOP AND GO, "OH, YEAH, RIGHT."

RICK BARBA: So once the script was complete, the story solid, and you got the puzzles in place, you moved into production mode. How involved were you?

LORELEI SHANNON: Pretty involved. I was on the set every day during the shooting. That was wonderful; it was a great opportunity. Most screenwriters don't get that chance.

RICK BARBA: Was it filmed in Seattle?

LORELEI SHANNON: Yes, in and around Seattle. Partly in a studio, and partly at various locations around Seattle.

An Annotated Walkthrough

RICK BARBA: What sort of locations? A lot of the game takes place inside WynTech and Curtis's apartment. Were those location shots?

LORELEI SHANNON: Those were sets. We had a wonderful set designer, Chris Klonecke, and his sets looked so cool. We did go to a couple of medical centers, and a restaurant which became the Dreaming Tree in the game. And we used a very cool-looking nightclub called The Weathered Wall.

RICK BARBA: Is that the Borderline in the game?

LORELEI SHANNON: Yes.

RICK BARBA: I didn't recognize any of the actors, but they did an awfully good job. Are they local? How did you cast it?

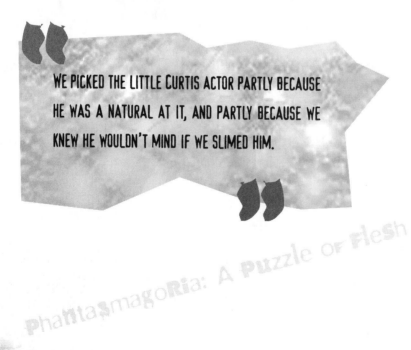

WE PICKED THE LITTLE CURTIS ACTOR PARTLY BECAUSE HE WAS A NATURAL AT IT, AND PARTLY BECAUSE WE KNEW HE WOULDN'T MIND IF WE SLIMED HIM.

A Conversation with Lorelei Shannon

LORELEI SHANNON: Some are local, some from Los Angeles. We arranged an open casting through various agents; we sent them character designs and asked them to find people who would work well. Again, some were local. The guy who played Curtis, in fact, is a local actor. I guess about a third of the actors came up from Los Angeles. It was very, very important to have good actors, because I feel this material is challenging and kind of intelligent. If we had bad actors doing this dramatic psychological stuff, it would just … suck.

RICK BARBA: (laughs) It was pretty intense material.

LORELEI SHANNON: I think our cast did quite well.

RICK BARBA: I do too. The actor who plays Curtis was well-cast—the perfect Everyman type of guy you can really identify with. So when the weird stuff starts to happen, it's all the more effective. And I thought the guy who played Trevor was great. Did he ad-lib much of his stuff, or was he pretty much on-script? All of his banter seemed so natural …

LORELEI SHANNON: Oh, he was pretty much on-script. He was just very, very good at the part. We were so pleased with him.

RICK BARBA: He's hilarious.

LORELEI SHANNON: He has great comic timing.

RICK BARBA: And I thought the camaraderie between Trevor and Curtis, so important in the story, felt entirely natural and believable.

An Annotated Walkthrough

LORELEI SHANNON: I'm glad. I was extremely pleased with both of them. They had to put up with so much. Especially Paul Morgan Stetler [who played Curtis], that poor guy. He was there every day. And because we had so many variables, we had to make him do so many things. I probably would have gone mad. And Paul Mitri [who played Trevor] was just delightful.

We ended up cutting quite a bit from the original script. The fellow who played Bob [Don Berg] had a lot of material eliminated. Which is too bad, because I thought he was wonderful, too.

RICK BARBA: Yeah, he was a good Bob.

LORELEI SHANNON: A terrific Bob. Actually a very sweet guy, but don't tell anyone. (laughs)

RICK BARBA: Tell us a shooting anecdote. People always love those behind-the-scenes stories.

LORELEI SHANNON: It was pretty hilarious when we hauled Paul Stetler off the bed by those chains. We actually used an enormous scissor-lift that was outside the set, hovering over us. We fired the thing up; it sounded like a tractor, and blew fumes everywhere. We'd haul the poor guy off the ground, do a take, then lower him back down. This went on for more than half a day. It was just so bizarre. It looked so surreal and interesting—and here's this giant machine on the other side of the wall, chugging away.

The stuff with the little boy [Curtis as a child] was a lot of fun. He's a very good little actor. He's our special effects man's son. We picked him partly because he was a natural at it, and partly because we knew he wouldn't mind if we slimed him. (laughs)

A Conversation with Lorelei Shannon

RICK BARBA: Yeah, I was going to ask you about the sliming process.

LORELEI SHANNON: Those were the hardest scenes to watch afterward. Those, and the scenes where the mom abuses the boy. Like, I wrote them, but I'd think, "Oh God, how could I do that?" And I was terribly afraid that I was going to traumatize him for life—but he didn't care.

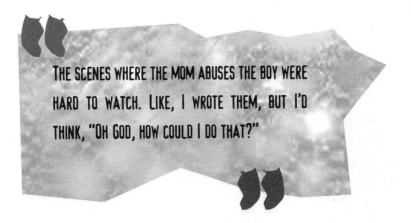

> THE SCENES WHERE THE MOM ABUSES THE BOY WERE HARD TO WATCH. LIKE, I WROTE THEM, BUT I'D THINK, "OH GOD, HOW COULD I DO THAT?"

RICK BARBA: Yeah, I've got a couple of sons myself, so I cringed extra hard at some of those scenes.

LORELEI SHANNON: Yeah, I bet. I've got my own little two-and-a-half-week-old beasty here.

RICK BARBA: Two-and-a-half weeks? Congratulations! Is it a boy?

LORELEI SHANNON: Yes, and he's the sweetest little thing.

[The interview temporarily disintegrates into about four minutes of parental gossip, advice, sentimental tale-swapping, and other unprintable exchanges.]

An Annotated Walkthrough

RICK BARBA: Now that *Phantasmagoria: A Puzzle of Flesh* is about to go gold this week, what's the next project for you?

LORELEI SHANNON: I don't really have anything scheduled at this point. It's all up in the air. Maybe I'll do something a little lighter. (laughs) Spending nearly two years in that incredibly dark world …

RICK BARBA: Just take your time.

LORELEI SHANNON: Yes, take a little time to hang out with the babe.

RICK BARBA: You know, with you joining Roberta Williams and Jane Jensen as a front-rank designer, Sierra is about the only company in the industry that features a lineup of female game designers. It's so great that Sierra presents that opportunity—as opposed to all the other "boy companies" with their *Doom* shooters and the like. It's refreshing to have intelligent, character-based games.

LORELEI SHANNON: Roberta Williams is a wonderful designer, and I learned so much from her. I really enjoyed our time together on *King's Quest VII*. She really is an amazing, supportive, wonderful person.

RICK BARBA: I've never met her, but I admire the direction she's pushed computer gaming. As a writer and a story-lover myself, I have great respect for her status as the Mother of Graphic Adventure Games.

LORELEI SHANNON: Yes. And she's every bit as neat as you might think she is. Very creative. We had the best time working together.

A Conversation with Lorelei Shannon

> PEOPLE STILL HAVE IT THOROUGHLY IMBEDDED IN THEIR HEADS THAT A "GAME" EQUALS "SOMETHING FOR CHILDREN." WHICH JUST ISN'T TRUE. THIS IS AN ADULT GAME.

RICK BARBA: I have to ask this. There's a lot of very adult material in *Phantasmagoria: A Puzzle of Flesh*, material that will probably cause quite a stir when the game releases.

> ALL OF THE ADULT MATERIAL IS INTEGRAL TO THE STORY. I DON'T THINK WE HAVE ANYTHING THAT'S GRATUITOUS OR PRURIENT—NO SEXUAL VIOLENCE, NO RAPE. NOTHING BEYOND WHAT YOU'D FIND IN AN R-RATED MOVIE.

LORELEI SHANNON: I think it will. But I think all of the adult material is integral to the story. I don't think we have anything that's gratuitous or prurient. I realize, however, that people still have it thoroughly imbedded in their heads that a "game" equals "something for children." Which just isn't true. This is an adult game. I've said it in just about every interview I've done. This game is not for children! I don't want anyone under 17 going anywhere near it. It's clearly labeled, and I sincerely hope people will pay attention to that.

An Annotated Walkthrough

The truth of the matter is, there's nothing in this game beyond what you'd find in an R-rated movie. We don't have any sexual violence; there's no rape or anything like that. But the story is very mature. I'd worry more about people being disturbed or unsettled by *Phantasmagoria 2*'s overall story and content than by individual incidents in the game.

RICK BARBA: Well, those disturbing, unsettling elements of the story were handled with sophistication and taste, I think.

LORELEI SHANNON: Yes, our director of photography, Matt Jensen, did an excellent job. And Andy Hoyos's direction was terrific.

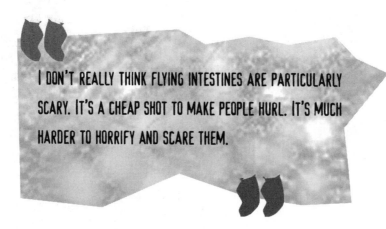

I DON'T REALLY THINK FLYING INTESTINES ARE PARTICULARLY SCARY. IT'S A CHEAP SHOT TO MAKE PEOPLE HURL. IT'S MUCH HARDER TO HORRIFY AND SCARE THEM.

RICK BARBA: Particularly those violent scenes. I noticed a focus on small details that suggested the horror and violence, rather than lingering on the blood and gore of the violent act itself.

A Conversation with Lorelei Shannon

LORELEI SHANNON: That's right. Our editor, Wes Plate, worked together with Andy to do some really good stuff. They created scenes that make you think you saw a whole lot more than you actually did. Which is what we were always aiming for. I don't really think flying intestines are particularly scary.

RICK BARBA: Playing scenes over and over again, as I have to do for a strategy guide, I noticed that. You don't really see too much grotesque violence in this game. So much is implied—which, of course, makes it all the more horrific.

LORELEI SHANNON: Yes, that's the way we intended it from the start. I think it's a cheap shot to make people hurl. (laughs) It's much harder to horrify and scare them.

Lorelei Shannon and Rick Barba
November 5, 1996

Prima
The World Leader in

Sid Meier's Civilization® II
The Official Strategy Guide

Leave your everlasting mark on civilization! Imagine what the world would be like if you could personally sculpt history from the dawn of time. Would you build the Roman Empire? Construct the Great Wall of China? Discover a cure for cancer? However you choose to rewrite history, don't make a single decision without consulting this guide.

$19.95
ISBN 1-7615-0106-1
By David Ellis

Duke Nukem 3D™
Unauthorized Game Secrets

You need more than pipebombs and true grit to make it out of L.A. alive and save the earth. What you need are the secrets in this guide. Inside you'll find, detailed maps for every mission, the locations of all secret areas, atom-smashing combat tactics, game-busting cheat codes, and much more.

$14.99
ISBN 0-7615-0783-3
By Michael van Mantgem and Kip Ward

WarCraft™ II
Beyond the Dark Portal
Official Secrets & Solutions

Only a fool would go wading through the fetid swamps of the Orcish homeland unprepared. Before you venture beyond the Dark Portal and into the twisted terrain of 24 new missions, you'd better have this guide. With this book's brutal strategies, you'll fit right in.

$14.99
ISBN 0-7615-0787-6
By Mark Walker

WarCraft™ II
Tides of Darkness
The Official Strategy Guide

No matter which side they choose, this guide will keep gamers on the victorious end of the pounding, pillaging, and plundering! From Zeppelins to Gryphon Riders, it's easy to build impermeable defenses and launch brutal assaults when you've got this book!

$19.95
ISBN 0-7615-0188-6
By Ed Dille

PRIMA'S
SECRETS
OF THE GAMES

Prima Publishing
PO Box 629000 • El Dorado Hills, CA 95762
To Order Call 1•800•531•2343

Secrets of the Games® is a registered trademark of Prima Publishing, a division of Prima Communications, Inc.

Publishing
Electronic Entertainment Books!

Ultimate Mortal Kombat™ 3
Official Arcade Secrets

The ultimate showdown awaits, and this guide is your ultimate source of UMK3 knowledge! It reveals ALL ultimate kombat kodes and hidden kontenders, blow-by-blow details to master all 22 kombatants, more than 300 killer kombos that will allow you to crush the opposition, and the lowdown on playing UMK3 on the Sega Saturn.

$9.99
ISBN 0-7615-0586-5
By Chris Rice and Simon Hill

Hexen™
The Official Strategy Guide

Enter the ultimate sword and sorcery battlefest that is Hexen! Destroy the Serpent Rider, and restore order to the Chronos dimension before it's too late! Whether players do battle as the mage, cleric, and fighter, this guide has what they need to complete their mission!

$19.95
ISBN 1-7615-0388-9
By Joe Bell Grant

Myst™
The Official Strategy Guide, Revised and Expanded Edition

In this #1 bestselling, ultimate, authoritative source for answers and information about Myst Island and the Ages of Myst, gamers will find a complete fictionalized walkthrough of Myst, detailed information about the many puzzles, screen images of the most important locations, and much more!

$19.95
ISBN 0-7615-0102-9
By Rick Barba and Rusel DeMaria

Prima's Sony PlayStation™ Game Secrets
The Unauthorized Edition Vol. 2

The Sony PlayStation is an electronic adrenaline rush of state-of-the-art gameplay, and this book is your definitive guide to all the pulse-pounding action. Whether you're into reflex-testing arcade games, martial arts mayhem, sports, war games, or role-playing, this compendium is packed with inside information you won't find anywhere else.

$12.99
ISBN 0-7615-0515-6
By Prima Creative Services, Vince Matthews, and Douglas R. Brumley

Computer Game Books

1942: The Pacific Air War—The Official Strategy Guide	$19.95
The 11th Hour: The Official Strategy Guide	$19.95
The 7th Guest: The Official Strategy Guide	$19.95
Aces Over Europe: The Official Strategy Guide	$19.95
Across the Rhine: The Official Strategy Guide	$19.95
Alone in the Dark 3: The Official Strategy Guide	$19.95
Armored Fist: The Official Strategy Guide	$19.95
Ascendancy: The Official Strategy Guide	$19.95
Buried in Time: The Journeyman Project 2—The Official Strategy Guide	$19.95
CD-ROM Games Secrets, Volume 1	$19.95
CD-ROM Games Secrets, Volume 2	$19.99
CD-ROM Classics	$19.99
Caesar II: The Official Strategy Guide	$19.95
Celtic Tales: Balor of the Evil Eye—The Official Strategy Guide	$19.95
Cyberia: The Official Strategy Guide	$19.95
Cyberia2: The Official Strategy Guide	$19.99
Dark Seed II: The Official Strategy Guide	$19.95
Descent: The Official Strategy Guide	$19.95
Descent II: The Official Strategy Guide	$19.99
DOOM Battlebook	$19.95
DOOM II: The Official Strategy Guide	$19.95
Dragon Lore: The Official Strategy Guide	$19.95
Dungeon Master II: The Legend of Skullkeep—The Official Strategy Guide	$19.95
Fleet Defender: The Official Strategy Guide	$19.95
Frankenstein: Through the Eyes of the Monster—The Official Strategy Guide	$19.95
Front Page Sports Football Pro '95: The Official Playbook	$19.95
Fury3: The Official Strategy Guide	$19.95
Hell: A Cyberpunk Thriller—The Official Strategy Guide	$19.95
Heretic: The Official Strategy Guide	$19.95
I Have No Mouth, and I Must Scream: The Official Strategy Guide	$19.95
In The 1st Degree: The Official Strategy Guide	$19.95
Kingdom: The Far Reaches—The Official Strategy Guide	$14.95
King's Quest VII: The Unauthorized Strategy Guide	$19.95
The Legend of Kyrandia: The Official Strategy Guide	$19.95
Lords of Midnight: The Official Strategy Guide	$19.95
Machiavelli the Prince: Official Secrets & Solutions	$12.95
Marathon: The Official Strategy Guide	$19.95
Master of Orion: The Official Strategy Guide	$19.95
Master of Magic: The Official Strategy Guide	$19.95
MechWarrior 2: The Official Strategy Guide	$19.95
Microsoft Arcade: The Official Strategy Guide	$12.95
Microsoft Flight Simulator 5.1: The Official Strategy Guide	$19.95
Microsoft Golf: The Official Strategy Guide	$19.95
Microsoft Space Simulator: The Official Strategy Guide	$19.95
Might and Magic Compendium:	
The Authorized Strategy Guide for Games I, II, III, and IV	$19.95
Mission Critical: The Official Strategy Guide	$19.95
Myst: The Official Strategy Guide	$19.95
Online Games: In-Depth Strategies and Secrets	$19.95
Oregon Trail II: The Official Strategy Guide	$19.95
Panzer General: The Official Strategy Guide	$19.95
Perfect General II: The Official Strategy Guide	$19.95
Prince of Persia: The Official Strategy Guide	$19.95
Prisoner of Ice: The Official Strategy Guide	$19.95
The Residents: Bad Day on the Midway— The Official Strategy Guide	$19.95
Return to Zork Adventurer's Guide	$14.95
Ripper: The Official Strategy Guide	$19.99

Romance of the Three Kingdoms IV: Wall of Fire—The Official Strategy Guide	$19.95
Shannara: The Official Strategy Guide	$19.95
Sid Meier's Civilization, or Rome on 640K a Day	$19.95
Sid Meier's Civilization II: The Official Strategy Guide	$19.99
Sid Meier's Colonization: The Official Strategy Guide	$19.95
SimCity 2000: Power, Politics, and Planning	$19.95
SimEarth: The Official Strategy Guide	$19.95
SimFarm Almanac: The Official Guide to SimFarm	$19.95
SimLife: The Official Strategy Guide	$19.95
SimTower: The Official Strategy Guide	$19.95
Stonekeep: The Official Strategy Guide	$19.95
SubWar 2050: The Official Strategy Guide	$19.95
Terry Pratchett's Discworld: The Official Strategy Guide	$19.95
Thunderscape: The Official Strategy Guide	$19.95
TIE Fighter Collector's CD-ROM: The Official Strategy Guide	$19.99
Under a Killing Moon: The Official Strategy Guide	$19.95
WarCraft: Orcs & Humans Official Secrets & Solutions	$9.95
WarCraft II: Tides of Darkness—The Official Strategy Guide	$19.99
Warlords II Deluxe: The Official Strategy Guide	$19.95
Werewolf Vs. Commanche: The Official Strategy Guide	$19.95
Wing Commander I, II, and III: The Ultimate Strategy Guide	$19.95
X-COM Terror From The Deep: The Official Strategy Guide	$19.95
X-COM UFO Defense: The Official Strategy Guide	$19.95
X-Wing Collector's CD-ROM: The Official Strategy Guide	$19.95

Video Game Books

3DO Game Guide	$16.95
Battle Arena Toshinden Game Secrets: The Unauthorized Edition	$12.95
Behind the Scenes at Sega: The Making of a Video Game	$14.95
Breath of Fire Authorized Game Secrets	$14.95
Breath of Fire II Authorized Game Secrets	$14.95
Complete Final Fantasy III Forbidden Game Secrets	$14.95
Donkey Kong Country Game Secrets the Unauthorized Edition	$9.95
Donkey Kong Country 2—Diddy's Kong Quest Unauthorized Game Secrets	$12.99
EA SPORTS Official Power Play Guide	$12.95
Earthworm Jim Official Game Secrets	$12.95
Earthworm Jim 2 Official Game Secrets	$14.95
GEX: The Official Power Play Guide	$14.95
Killer Instinct Game Secrets: The Unauthorized Edition	$9.95
Killer Instinct 2 Unauthorized Arcade Secrets	$12.99
The Legend of Zelda: A Link to the Past—Game Secrets	$12.95
Lord of the Rings Official Game Secrets	$12.95
Maximum Carnage Official Game Secrets	$9.95
Mortal Kombat II Official Power Play Guide	$9.95
Mortal Kombat 3 Official Arcade Secrets	$9.95
Mortal Kombat 3 Official Power Play Guide	$9.95
NBA JAM: The Official Power Play Guide	$12.95
Ogre Battle: The March of the Black Queen—The Official Power Play Guide	$14.95
Parent's Guide to Video Games	$12.95
PlayStation Game Secrets: The Unauthorized Edition, Vol. 1	$12.99
Secret of Evermore: Authorized Power Play Guide	$12.95
Secret of Mana Official Game Secrets	$14.95
Street Fighter Alpha—Warriors' Dreams Unauthorized Game Secrets	$12.99
Ultimate Mortal Kombat 3 Official Arcade Secrets	$9.99
Urban Strike Official Power Play Guide, with Desert Strike & Jungle Strike	$12.95

To Order Books

Please send me the following items:

Quantity	Title	Unit Price	Total
_____	_____	$ _____	$ _____
_____	_____	$ _____	$ _____
_____	_____	$ _____	$ _____
_____	_____	$ _____	$ _____
_____	_____	$ _____	$ _____

Subtotal $ _____

Deduct 10% when ordering 3-5 books $ _____

7.25% Sales Tax (CA only) $ _____

8.25% Sales Tax (TN only) $ _____

5.0% Sales Tax (MD and IN only) $ _____

Shipping and Handling* $ _____

Total Order $ _____

Shipping and Handling depend on Subtotal.

Subtotal	Shipping/Handling
$0.00–$14.99	$3.00
$15.00–$29.99	$4.00
$30.00–$49.99	$6.00
$50.00–$99.99	$10.00
$100.00–$199.99	$13.50
$200.00+	Call for Quote

Foreign and all Priority Request orders:
Call Order Entry department
for price quote at 916/632-4400

This chart represents the total retail price of books only
(before applicable discounts are taken).

By Telephone: With MC or Visa, call 800-632-8676, 916-632-4400. Mon-Fri, 8:30-4:30.
WWW {http://www.primapublishing.com}

Orders Placed Via Internet E-mail {sales@primapub.com}

By Mail: Just fill out the information below and send with your remittance to:

Prima Publishing
P.O. Box 1260BK
Rocklin, CA 95677

My name is _____

I live at _____

City_____ State_____ Zip _____

MC/Visa#_____ Exp._____

Check/Money Order enclosed for $_____ Payable to Prima Publishing

Daytime Telephone _____

Signature _____